AuthorHouse™ UK
1663 Liberty Drive
Bloomington, IN 47403 USA
www.authorhouse.co.uk
Phone: 0800.197.4150

Published by AuthorHouse 01/09/2019

ISBN: 978-1-7283-8263-0 (sc)
ISBN: 978-1-7283-8262-3 (e)

Print information available on the last page.

This book is printed on acid-free paper.

authorHOUSE®

'These boots were made for walking - but I am not so sure about my feet !'

"This book is a compilation of details of six walks in an area of North Staffordshire, outlined with directions and accompanied with hand drawn maps, along with many photographs I have taken along the routes. Added to this, with each walk, is a series of internet research 'topics of interest' that look at historical information related to the area of each walk. The book is the first part of a personal project that seeks to 'discover' interesting facts about the county of 'Staffordshire' whilst enjoying the health benefits of a pleasant scenic walk in the fresh country air".

DISCOVERING STAFFORDSHIRE

An Historical Companion Guide

To Walking In North Staffordshire

Contents

WALKING IN NORTH STAFFORDSHIRE   -   Outline Details of the Walks

Walk GM01   **Danebridge to Gradbach**

Start point :-	Distance	approximately - 6 miles (9.5 km.)
OS Grid Ref.	Time taken for walk	4 hours and 45 minutes.
SJ 96447 65218	Elevation (c. 500 feet)	(Start - Danebridge – c. 600 ft.)
	Highest point	(Roaches Ridge – c. 1100 ft.)

Walk GM02   **Flash Village and Three Shire Heads**

Start point :-	Distance	approximately - 4 miles (6.5 km.)
OS Grid Ref.	Time taken for walk	3 hours.
SK 03201 67863	Elevation (c. 600 feet)	(Start–Flash Bar(Oliver Hill)c.1650ft.)
	Lowest point	(Knar Farm - c.1050 ft.)

Walk GM03   **Rushton Spencer and Cloudside**

Start point :-	Distance	approximately – 5 miles (8 km.)
OS Grid Ref.	Time taken for walk	3 hours.
SJ 93625 62405	Elevation (c. 400 feet)	(Start – Rushton Spencer – c. 500 ft.)
	Highest point	(Cloudside – c.900 ft.)

Walk GM04   **Rushton Spencer to Whitelee Weir**

Start point :-	Distance	approximately – 5 miles (8km.)
OS Grid Ref.	Time taken for walk	3 hours and 30 minutes.
SJ 93625 62405	Elevation (c. 300 feet)	(Start - Rushton Spencer – c. 500 ft.)
	Highest point	(Heaton – c. 800 ft.)

Walk GM05   **Winking Man, Dove Head and Hollinsclough**

Start point :-	Distance	approximately - 8 ¾ miles (14 km.)
OS Grid Ref.	Time taken for walk	6 hours.
SK 02455 63635	Elevation (c. 600 feet)	(Start – Morridge – c. 1500 ft.)
	Lowest point	(Hollinsclough - c. 900 ft.)

Walk GM06   **Longnor Village**

Start point :-	Distance	approximately - 4 ½ miles (7 km.)
OS Grid Ref.	Time taken for walk	3 hours and 30 minutes.
SK 08370 65617	Elevation (c. 200 feet)	(Start - Longnor Edge – c. 1050 ft.)
	Lowest point	(Glutton Bridge – c. 850 ft.)

INTRODUCTION

Whenever you go walking, do you ever look at the buildings along the way and think of the history behind them? Having an artistic eye, I also relate to the design of the buildings and their aesthetic qualities, probably more so than the actual purpose that they were built for. Looking at churches for example, though I am not a church-goer myself, I can appreciate the time and effort that has been taken to build even some of the more basic religious buildings. I suppose this comes from having some Christian and moral values, but my interest is more of an artistic nature, just as it is when I am out walking in the countryside. I let my imagination take me into a world of adventure and wonder, as I consider the differences between what I see today and what may have been there many years before.

Whilst I was compiling the historical information sections of topics of interest, they became more of an educational inspiration to me than simply being alongside a record of my walks. It also dawned on me that many people who set out for walks must have similar views to my own, and I set out a plan for the book to be used as a companion guide, especially for those who were perhaps taking a walking holiday in the area. At the same time, it is possible to read the book without actually doing any of the walking and hopefully still appreciate the history of each area.

There are six walks in this book, but some could be done in parts, and some could be done together, one after the other. My own initial thoughts were to provide some details of six walks for six days of a holiday in the North Staffordshire Moorlands area, but, in some ways, it barely shows the true beauty and identity of a part of the country in which I was born. I chose Staffordshire as a limitation to my walking endeavours as I was born and bred in Staffordshire, yet even now I am finding things out that I had no knowledge of from the past. I have no doubt that millions of people in this country would have similar experiences to my own if they were to venture out and search the history of their own 'county' of origin.

When I first started writing this 'booklet', as it was meant to be, it was with the intention of setting down a simple record of my exploits of 'walking in Staffordshire'. The initial research that I did into the planning of the walks, and the subsequent discoveries of unplanned sights along the routes that I took, soon turned the whole idea into something like a large school project. I do not apologise for this fact, as it has been a very interesting experience for myself, but my booklet has now developed more into something resembling a 'text book', yet one which I hope will be regarded as a companion guide to walkers and ramblers in Staffordshire.

The idea of making a record of some walks in Staffordshire had been on my mind since taking a short break to the Lake District a few years ago with my wife. We had decided to follow in the footsteps of some famous names, including my wife's sister and her husband, (that's Mr. and Mrs. Smith to everyone else), who are regular walkers. The inspiration behind my thoughts of writing about my own exploits began after reading a nice little book that we had bought in Ambleside. The name of this book was – 'Walking with Wordsworth in the Lake District'.

I had already been interested in the scenic qualities of some areas of Staffordshire as I have driven through many quaint villages around the county and made many mental notes over the years. Being moderately artistically inclined and having a hobby of drawing and painting various subjects, it was one of my initial intentions to find interesting landscapes and old church buildings as subject material. With a little historic interest added to my thoughts, and having read the 'Wordsworth' book, I decided to keep a record of my ventures into the Staffordshire countryside. The planning of my walks involved studying map books for marked footpaths, especially from village church to village church, as well as looking for general places of interest and listed buildings such as great halls, grand farmhouses and old pubs. Geographical features such as rivers, hills and rock formations all came into the mix, along with some interesting animals encountered. Initial research on the internet gave me a deeper insight and interest in features that I had seen on my walks and some topics gave rise to warranting further investigation. The more I searched, the greater my interest level became. When topics of legends, saints and knights, amongst all manner of general knowledge, began to unfold, my walks became a bit more interesting than just putting one foot in front of the other.

The planning of each walk however, was much easier on paper than it was in the field, pun intended, as trying to locate footpaths at ground level that actually headed in the right direction was quite difficult at times. So, it was to be an interesting journey each time I embarked on one of my ventures, but, even armed with a rough idea of where I wanted to go, and what I wanted to see, it was a little 'unsurprising' that some parts of each journey did not turn out the way it was supposed to. My first outing with my wife didn't exactly inspire confidence, with slipping on wet mossy rocks whilst trying to cross Black Brook near Gradbach certainly not helping matters. I strived to keep up an interest level in future planning of walks for my wife's benefit, in the hope that she would join me again on my intrepid adventures, which came with small chunks of uncertainty but also with rewards of pleasant surprises amongst the mishaps and disappointments. So, it began with a trek from Danebridge village, up the eastern bank of the River Dane and an exploration into what became a mission to find out the 'secrets' of Staffordshire.

There are six walks in this edition, some short and some long, some more physically demanding than others, but in all of them I have tried to give an account of a simple walk with a reflection of the past, by accumulating an assortment of historical information that was part of the local development over time. With each walk I have also tried to find an information link from one walk to the next, in an attempt to give some continuity throughout the book, but each walk has some interesting topics included in its own entity.

Although these are my own personal recollections of my walks in my birth county of Staffordshire, (as Walsall was in Staffordshire when I was born), hopefully they are of interest to anyone who wishes to read about them. I have included most of my investigations into places of interest from various internet sites as part of the appeal to a walk in unfamiliar territory, so I hope you enjoy the account of my explorations, and in some ways, as I have, gain a new education in the subject of 'rambling' in the North Staffordshire Moorlands.

Guy Madeley   (2015)

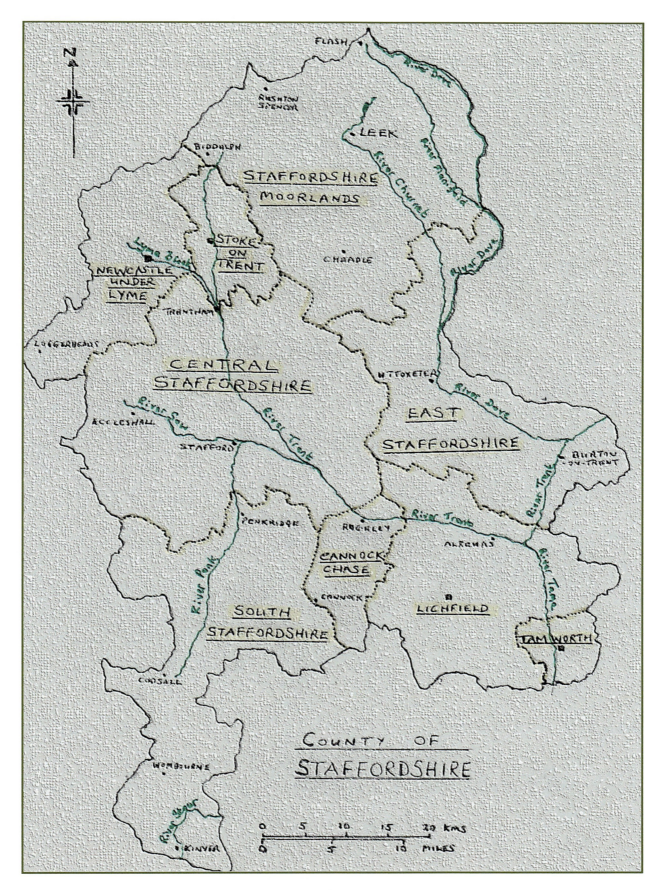

Map of the county of Staffordshire – showing nine districts

Location Map Of Six Walks In The North Staffordshire Moorlands

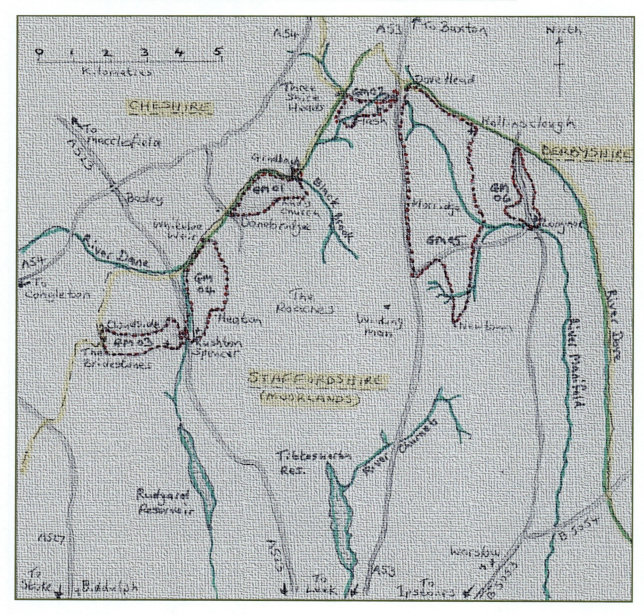

Walk GM01   Danebridge to Gradbach

Walk GM02   Flash Village and Three Shire Heads

Walk GM03   Rushton Spencer and Cloudside

Walk GM04   Rushton Spencer to Whitelee Weir

Walk GM05   Winking Man, Dove Head and Hollinsclough

Walk GM06   Longnor Village

DISCOVERING STAFFORDSHIRE

An Historical Companion Guide

To Walking In North Staffordshire

Danebridge to Gradbach

(Walk No. GM01 – March)

View of Danebridge Methodist Church and the River Dane

The plans for my first walk involved starting from the village of Danebridge, at the bridge crossing the River Dane and the village 'chapel' as my initial viewing points. Then I had decided to aim to see the chapel in the village of Gradbach further up the river. Strangely, the chapel of Gradbach is located on the Cheshire bank of the river, yet the village itself is nearly half a mile downstream on the Staffordshire bank. My next point of call was to be, as it is now called, 'Luds Church'. This is a small rock cleft, or gorge, which intrigued me because of its unusual formation, and its possible link to a knight's legend that sees Lud's Church as a possible location of the medieval poem's 'Green Chapel' in 'Sir Gawain and the Green Knight'. It is also reputed to have been a hiding place for both Robin Hood and Bonny Prince Charlie in some records. I then made a detour to the top of the 'Roaches' ridge and was rewarded with a glorious view across the Staffordshire Moorlands, before coming back down from the ridge to find the 'Hanging Stone', a strange rock outcrop in the hillside not far from Swythamley, near to Danebridge. At the end of the walk I couldn't resist the temptation to cross back over the bridge into Wincle village, which is less than one hundred yards into Cheshire, and had a brief look at the Ship Inn. I also visited the Wincle Brewery where I allowed myself to buy some of the local beers for a well - deserved refreshing drink when I got home.

My internet investigations had given me a mental picture of how Danebridge village, the bridge, and the surrounding environment histories had unfolded, and, with some recent modern additions in historical terms, this made for a more interesting walk I thought. From a humble river crossing in the beginning, a hamlet had emerged, with working mills for community employment. The addition of a place of worship in 1834, in the form of a Methodist church, made Danebridge a complete village. The surrounding communities that sprang up became part of the formation of what were known as 'townships'. This walk traverses across three townships, which has Danebridge in the township of Heaton. Gradbach was in the township of Quarnford, with the area known as 'Leekfrith' township in between.

My walk also put me in the vicinity of more recent buildings, including Back Dane Cottage, which is a converted farmhouse now used as a weekend retreat for underprivileged children, and Back Forest Flocks Farm which breeds rare sheep. Gradbach Mill has been converted more than once since it was built c.1760, and other mills in Danebridge and Wincle had been grinding corn from local farms since 1652. They were used for making a variety of cloths, and paper, in later industrial periods.

Old ancient bridleways and pathways may have disappeared, but there are numerous, more recently established public footpaths that have emerged to help explore our countryside. Though some footpaths are easier to follow than others, the exploration of the unknown has been made a lot easier for me at least. There have also been a few re-drawings of my maps along the way, which will hopefully make life easier for anyone wishing to follow in the footsteps of my investigations, which have become more of an 'educational mission'.

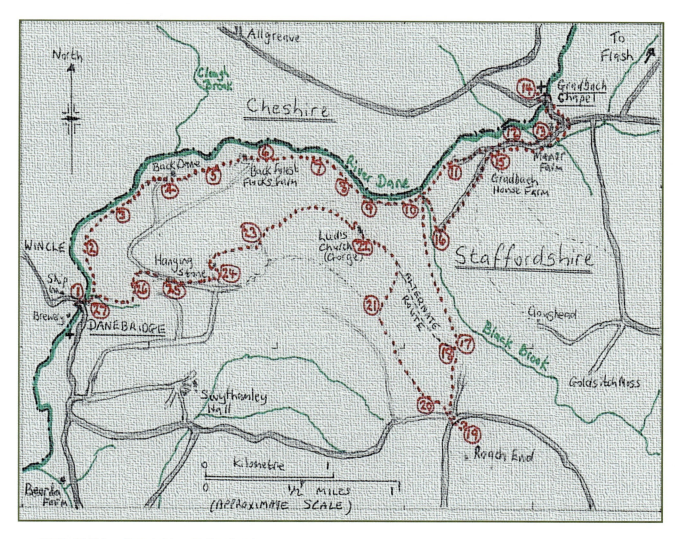

Walk GM01 - Danebridge to Gradbach

<u>Walk Reference – GM 01</u>   <u>Danebridge Chapel to Gradbach Chapel</u>

Drive to the start point (Grid Ref. SJ 96447 65218) using the A54 Congleton to Buxton road; travel from Congleton, then, after the Bosley crossroads and about a further 3 miles on the road to Buxton, turn right at the signpost for Wincle and the "Ship Inn". Follow the road downhill for about two miles until you reach the bridge of Danebridge just past the "Ship Inn" in Wincle, where you can park at the roadside, though this is limited at busy times.

<u>Walk Details</u>

Starting in the village of Danebridge, Staffordshire, then up along the east bank of the River Dane to Gradbach Mill and then slightly further upriver to Gradbach Chapel.

- Returning via Black Brook, Gradbach Wood, Roaches End Ridge, "Lud's Church" gorge and the Hanging Stone, then back to Danebridge.

The walk is about 6 miles long and takes about 4 and ¾ hours to complete, with some strenuous uphill climbs. Underfoot it is slippery, muddy and rocky, along with numerous patches of tree roots, which makes it difficult terrain to negotiate at times.

(Please note : - no real toilet facilities except at the Ship Inn, with permission as required).

1) – From the bridge at Danebridge, you can see the River Dane below and looking to the right there is a view of Danebridge Methodist church just above the river. I had a brief walk around the church in the quiet village before heading back to the bridge. Just on the Staffordshire side of the bridge there is a large gate with a signpost for "Gradbach 2¼ m, via Dane Valley". You can climb over the fence at the side of the gate, which puts you onto a wide muddy path by the River Dane.

2) – Start walking along the muddy path and note almost immediately on your right, a stream and stile leading to an uphill pathway which will be the end of the walk later. Continue on with the muddy path along the River Dane, going through a small gateway after about 200 metres, which has a marker on it labelled 'Staffordshire Council', where you continue on a grass pathway until you pass a metal gate on your left and alongside a wired fence slightly uphill to another small wooden gate.

3) – Go through the gate and then turn left here, negotiating a few wooden steps and then a muddy pathway which continues uphill into a wooded area. This has some wooden boarded sections amongst muddy patches. Continue on, both uphill and downhill for about 800 metres until you reach a stile. Climb over the stile, where you will see a stone wall on your right and some gorse bushes.

4) – Continue along the clear pathway for about 250 metres, when it meets a wide track/drive. Also, on the left is a house with a large wooden gate, this is "Back Dane Cottage", but do not go through the gate.
(For more information about Back Dane Cottage, go to its website – www.backdane.co.uk)

   *- Walk time, approximately 30 minutes so far.

Back Dane Cottage

5) – Walking on past Back Dane, the drive/track goes slightly uphill, where a left fork takes you onto a grass pathway marked with a post. After 200 metres the path narrows between gorse bushes, a bit rocky in places, then continue to a grass path where the River Dane can be seen to your left down the hillside. The pathway continues on to a stone wall which has a gap and broken fencing beside a stile. A few rocks here and a small stream to cross, then continue for a further 250 metres to another stile.

6) – Here the pathway goes between two fields, which are wire fenced, and a short distance ahead you will see a farm house and buildings, which are part of the Rare Sheep Breeding Farm known as "Back Forest Flocks". The pathway continues through a small gateway and over a stile.
(For more information about Back Forest Flocks, go to its website – www.backforest.co.uk)

Back Forest Flocks Farm

7) – Sign posts on this path section are marked with "Dane Valley Way" or "DVW", and the path continues between fields with wire fences slightly downhill to a wooded area closer to the river. Looking on your left, the river has rock cliffs above it, about 40 feet high, with the steep hillside on the Cheshire side towering above. Another stile, then the track continues into woodland with lots of muddy patches to negotiate.

*- Walk time, approximately 45 minutes now.

8) – Another stile, more muddy patches, tree roots and rocky areas continue for a further 400 metres or more, with both uphill and downhill sections. Then the pathway descends closer to the riverbank where good views of rocks and white water in the river make a scenic view (see following pictures).

9) – The pathway continues through woodland, uphill and downhill, with tree roots, rocks, and more mud patches to negotiate for about 400 metres, until track meets up with a sign post on another path which shows a marker pointing in the direction you have just come from, "Danebridge". Veer left here to continue, where you then come to an area of tree roots and pathways in four directions. You will see a small foot bridge on your left.

River Dane cliffs near Back Forest Flocks Farm

River Dane – near to the footbridge at the Black Brook tributary

Footbridge over Black Brook, where it meets the River Dane

10) - Cross over the footbridge of Black Brook, then go over the stile or through the gap in the fence, which has been signposted "Gradbach". Veer right slightly uphill here to a gap in the stone wall on your left. There are a few stone steps to negotiate here too.

   *- Walk time, approximately 1hr. 10 mins. up to now.

11) – Through the wall, you will see a drive/track bending left and right. Go left, down towards the River Dane, along a well-trodden very muddy pathway, until you reach a gate with a gap between two large upright stones to your right. Squeeze through here then turn left along another muddy pathway that will soon bring you into view with Gradbach Mill.

Gradbach Mill – now an outdoor pursuits centre for Newcastle under Lyme College

View of the river Dane, and tributary fork, near Manor Farm at Gradbach

Stream opposite Manor Farm, Gradbach, just before it reaches the River Dane

12) – Having come through a small gateway/stile to the pathway for the mill, continue towards the mill building, then veer right, walking up the driveway which then veers left uphill to a small road. At the end of the driveway you turn left, though note on the right a sign pointing to "Gradbach Scout Camp", which will act as a bearing on the return journey shortly.

13) – Firstly though, a small detour to see Gradbach chapel, which for some reason is on the Cheshire side of the river only a short walk away. Following the road downhill, you will come to the car park provided by Staffordshire County Council for walkers. Walking through the car park you will see a footpath, marked with "DVW" for Dane Valley Way, and the path comes to a fork in the river. The left fork being the River Dane, but a footbridge takes you over the right fork tributary stream and back to the road. Walking on the road, over a small road bridge, the stream is on your right where opposite Manor Farm buildings to your left, the stream becomes golden in colour from an adjoining stream.

14) – Walking up past Manor Farm to a larger road, turn left, you will notice another sign for Gradbach Scout Camp. (Turning right here the road would take you to Flash village). Turning left, the road bends around behind a house on the hillside to your right, and the River Dane comes back to you on your left. After about 200 metres you will come to a road bridge into Cheshire over the River Dane, where the Wesleyan Gradbach chapel, dated on the building as 1849, is before you.

*- Walk time, approximately 1hr. 45 mins.

(Time for your sandwich break, then get ready for the 'strenuous' return journey)

Gradbach Chapel, dated 1849, Wesleyan Methodist building on the Cheshire bank of the River Dane

15) – Firstly, starting from Gradbach Chapel, retrace your steps all the way back to the top of the driveway of Gradbach Mill, where the sign pointing to Gradbach Scout Camp was first noted. Go left here, taking the road which goes up past the scout buildings on your right, where you will come to Gradbach House Farm on your left. The farm is gated and has a stile on the right-hand side. There is a pathway beyond this over the stile which goes to Flash village, but you should continue with the track to the right and head down a wide drive/track, slightly muddy in places, which goes back towards Black Brook. Where the track bears left, with the stone wall on your right bearing right with a downhill grass pathway, you can choose either pathway, but beware!!! If you go left to the brook, a crossing of very slippery rocks awaits you (note; unfortunately, my wife slipped and fell into Black Brook here days before). The safer path is to descend to the right heading back down to the footbridge taken earlier, then crossing the brook safely and taking the left turn at the four-way sign post you can walk back up to this other 'dangerous' crossing point.

Gradbach House Farm

16) – From the slippery stones crossing point of Black Brook, the path is very steep uphill. Follow the signs for the "Roaches", where you will have to negotiate some very muddy patches, rocky outcrops and tree roots. Bear right after about 150 metres uphill, veering away from the brook now disappearing from view below.

17) - The path follows yellow markers further uphill for more than 400 metres, where the path levels slightly with more muddy patches, before rising again steeply to the top of the ridge almost another 400 metres. Then a final push uphill to the top of the hill where you will come to a signpost, where after a breather, you continue up to the "Roaches".

   *- Walk time, approximately 45 mins. returning, - but total time now 2hrs.30mins.

18) – As an alternative route, you can turn right here and have a relatively flat walk through muddy woodland to go directly to "Lud's Church", which is actually a small gorge, and not a church.

   However, a more scenic reward will be found at the top of the "Roaches", but the pain barrier is tested as you climb further uphill, through very muddy patches.

19) – The less muddy route up to the Roaches is to keep as close to the stone wall on your left as possible. Finally, you reach another stone wall with another stile and immediately left there are some stone steps through a gap in the wall. Walk over the road by Roach End Farm, then go up the rising ground to the rock formations above. From here you get a glorious view of Tittesworth reservoir in the distance, with Leek town beyond that almost in view.

Tittesworth reservoir view from Roaches End

20) – Head back down the hill to the stone wall, where the gap has a signpost pointing straight ahead for Lud's Church and Swythamley. Over a stile with the stone wall on your left a good track ahead takes you across the top of the "Ridge". After about 450 metres or more, the track forks, where you take the right fork for "Lud's Church".

21) – The pathway goes downhill to another signpost, where you go right for Lud's Church steeply downhill, and is slightly awkward underfoot in places. Watch out for possibly twisting your ankles and proceed fairly slowly here. After about 400 metres downhill it meets a wooded area which becomes very muddy, and a three-way signpost. Right for Gradbach, which is the track suggested earlier as the alternative pathway, or left here takes us to our goal, "Lud's Church" gorge.

*- Walk time now approximately 3 hours in total.

22) – The pathway goes through some very muddy patches, with trees and shrubs making footing very difficult, for about 200 metres or more. You reach a signpost pointing left, with a glimpse of the rock cleft to your right. A steep drop into the cleft is not advised here, but about 20 metres further on, a slightly easier descent is achievable on your right. At the bottom of the descent be aware of very muddy patches as you continue into the rock formation known as "Lud's Church".

"Lud's Church" – rock cleft formation

*- Walk time, approximately 3hrs. 45 mins. now in total.

23) – Coming out of Lud's Church, you will come to a three-way signpost. Follow the path left to "Swythamley". A decent pathway at first becomes muddy in places but continues for about 500 metres to another signpost near a farm gate. Again, head for Swythamley, but after only 25 metres or so, look to the right where a signpost points across the field. You will have to climb up some rock steps to read the sign for "Hanging Stone – Concession Path". A grass pathway lies ahead across the field, where you will find a broken gate at a stone wall, with rock steps to cross a ditch here into the next field section. The grass pathway continues when all of a sudden you see a large rock jutting out on the downward slope. This is known as the "Hanging Stone", and if you descend the steps underneath, it might become clear as to why it has this name. I think it may have been used to throw a rope over it to hang people in the past, but I have found no evidence of this in my research as yet.

Hanging Stone – near Swythamley

24) – Going underneath the stone to the right brings you to some steps and a steep downhill pathway to a road/ driveway below, where there is a cattle grid and stile with a signpost for the "Concession Path". At this point, head right along the driveway towards a farm building on your right. This is Hangingstone Farm.

Hangingstone Farm – and path to Danebridge

25) – At the farm, you will see another stile on your left, with the signpost for "Danebridge". Climb over the stile and continue across the field to the next stile and a field that has some sheep in it. Continue across the field where you will see a wooded area and then another stile comes into view.

26) - Climb over this stile and be aware of some steep steps downhill into the wooded area where a stream trickles down on your right. Further downhill, an adjoining stream is crossed by a wooden bridge boarding, then a signpost with a white marker is seen at a fork in the path. It should be obvious to fork right to continue to Danebridge but watch out for more muddy patches here.

River Dane – near to the bridge at Danebridge – (and the end of the walk).

27) – Near the bottom of the pathway you have to step over a small stream, about a foot wide, to finally get down back to Danebridge where you will see the River Dane at the point where you started from – about 4hrs. 45 minutes earlier.

   *- Walk time, approximately 4hrs. 45 mins. in total.

HISTORICAL COMPANION GUIDE TOPICS   -   WALK GM01

1.1 Danebridge Village   - A Brief History

1.2 Townships

1.3 Soay and Boreray   -   Rare Breeds of Sheep at Back Forest Flocks

1.4 Mills on the River Dane   - Gradbach Mill

1.5 Lud's 'Church'   - Sir Gawain and the Green Knight

The River Dane

1.1 *Danebridge Village - A Brief History

Danebridge village lies next to the River Dane, on a route of an ancient pathway which ran between Leek and Macclesfield called 'The Hollow Way'. The pathway was used by monks from Dieu La Cresse (now called Dieulacres) Abbey, near Leek, to carry wool by packhorse to markets in Macclesfield and beyond. It passed over Gun Hill, then to Swythamley, and to Danebridge to cross the River Dane. The pathway continued through Wincle and Clulow Cross to Macclesfield. It was also used to transport salt and iron from the Peak district mines.

A crossing point over the River Dane was recorded in 1190 as Scliderford, meaning 'slippery ford', crossing the river from Staffordshire into Cheshire. A bridge was recorded there in 1357, and in 1545 it was known as Sliderford Bridge. This was rebuilt in the early 17th century with a stone bridge having two arches, but this was washed away by a flood in 1631. The following year, the bridge was replaced with a single arched bridge, which was probably similar to the present bridge which was built as a replacement in 1869.

Bridge of 1869 at Danebridge, Staffordshire, over the River Dane

The bridge that stands today in Danebridge was built in 1869, and was listed as a grade 2 structure on 14 June 1984 with the following description -

– "Roadbridge, 1869, of reddish-buff rock faced gritstone. One deep segmented arch of substantial span. Battered buttresses at inner ends of abutments. Projecting smooth bands at road level support plain ashlar parapets. The corners beneath the arch are chamfered. Date on keystone. The south abutment is in Heaton C.P. Staffordshire." –

The bridge was funded by the two counties of Staffordshire and Cheshire, each giving £1,000 towards the costs of building, whereas the land and materials for the bridge were donated by Mr. John Brocklehurst, the landowner from nearby Swythamley Hall.

There was a house recorded at the river crossing at Danebridge in 1708, and the 'hamlet', as it was then, developed in the late 18th and early 19th centuries in association with a cotton mill built there. Religious guidance, in the form of Methodist services took place in Danebridge village on alternate Sundays from 1798, which were held in the cotton mill from 1806. A Wesleyan Methodist chapel was opened at Danebridge in 1834, which was on the site where the chapel stands today, and in so doing the 'hamlet' of Danebridge became a 'village'.

Danebridge Methodist Church

It is now recognised by many that the definition of a village is that of a settlement that has a church or chapel as a place for religious worship, whereas a settlement without a church may be considered a hamlet. So, in 1841, the population of Danebridge 'village', with its newly built chapel, was recorded in the census as just over 50 inhabitants. In 1851, on census Sunday, the attendance in the chapel was recorded as 80 in the afternoon, and 120 in the evening - which included all the children in the village. The chapel has been known as the Danebridge Methodist Church since 1991.

1.2 *Townships

In many areas of England, the basic unit name of an area of civil administration was the 'parish', and generally identified by the fact that it was linked with the church of that area. However, that was not always the case, as particularly found in northern England, there was a smaller unit called a 'township', usually being a subdivision of a parish.

Townships appointed members of the community as overseers of the poor and surveyors of highways, in a similar way to the parish system. They financed their obligations by levying a tax rate, probably similar to the council tax system of today. Most townships disappeared before 1866, as they were either included into adjacent civil parishes or gained their own separate civil parish status.

The use of the term 'township' still persisted after this and has been revived in some parts of northern England as a name for subdivisions of council boroughs.

Generally, the 'township' was reference to the area where the control of the tax and legal administration of a 'rural' community was overseen. This did not always mean that there was a governing body in that township, but may refer to a manor, or chapelry, or church parish council. Many townships became civil parishes in their own name, and it is interesting to note that the original definition of a Civil Parish, (or CP), was – "any place, in respect of which, that a tax rate could lawfully be levied".

Townships of the Danebridge area walk

Danebridge village lies on the north-west boundary of an area formerly known as a 'township' in the parish of Leek. The township was known as Heaton, with the hamlet of Heaton itself in the south of the area which was to become a civil parish of Staffordshire. I refer to Heaton as a 'hamlet' on the basis it has no place of worship in the settlement.

Heaton, which is an old English name meaning 'high settlement', stands at approximately 800 feet above sea level. However, this is quite low compared to the village of Flash, which lies in the neighbouring township of Quarnford not more than 5 miles away at 1518 feet. Flash is reputed to be the highest village in England. The highest point in the township of Heaton is the hill named 'Gun' in the east, rising to approximately 1,000 feet, with Danebridge village itself in the River Dane valley standing at 617 feet above sea level.

The walk from Danebridge to Gradbach lies within the 'parish' of Leek, which had at one time some nineteen separate 'townships' in its domain. My walk goes through parts of three of these, starting in 'Heaton township' at Danebridge, then through 'Leekfrith township' from Back Forest Farm to Black Brook, and then into 'Quarnford township' for Gradbach.

It is interesting to note that Heaton 'hamlet' itself has no church or chapel, but does have Heaton Hall Farm, which may have been the centre of administration for the township. The township may have been administered possibly from Swythamley Hall, which had the Brocklehurst family residing there as the landowners and who were responsible for the provision of building materials for the bridge at Danebridge.

The main village of Leekfrith township, having two places of worship with St. Matthews church and a Methodist chapel, is 'Meerbrook'. I assume that this was the centre of administration for the township, but I plan to visit this at a later time so more information may be gleaned then.

The township of Quarnford has its main village as Flash, which is the main focal point of my next walk. It also has Gradbach within its boundaries, but not the chapel at Gradbach which sits on the Cheshire bank of the River Dane. I have yet to find out if the Methodist chapel came under the domain of the township, or whether that was the reason it was built there.

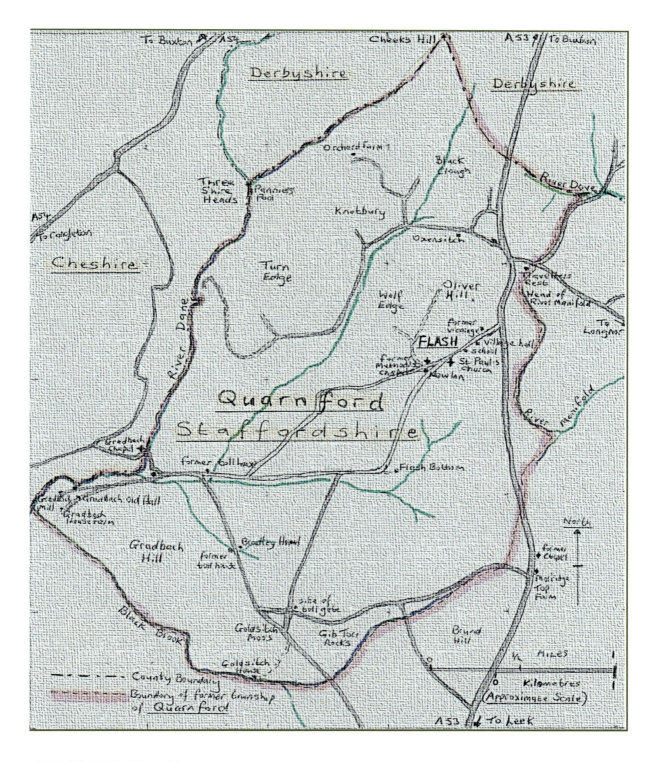

Map of Quarnford Township

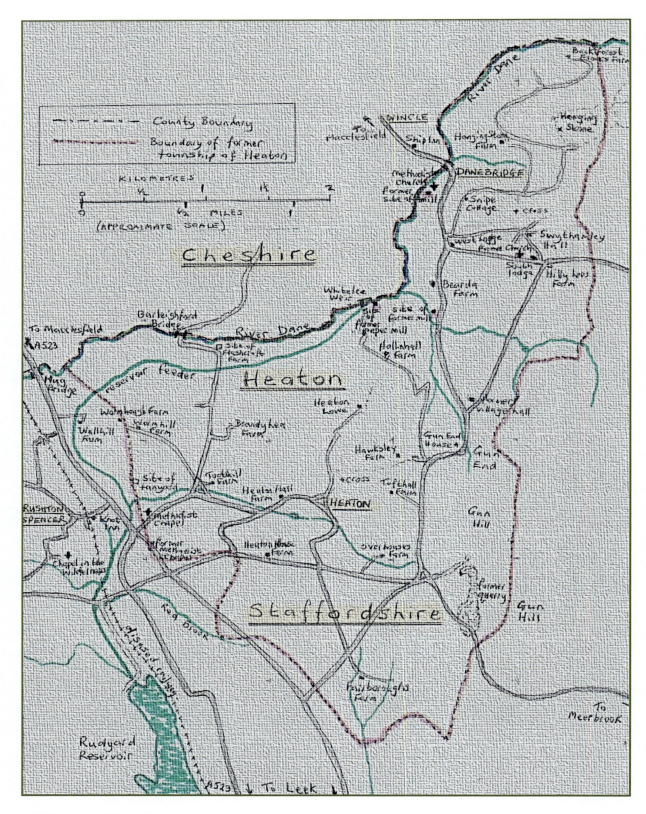

Map of Heaton Township

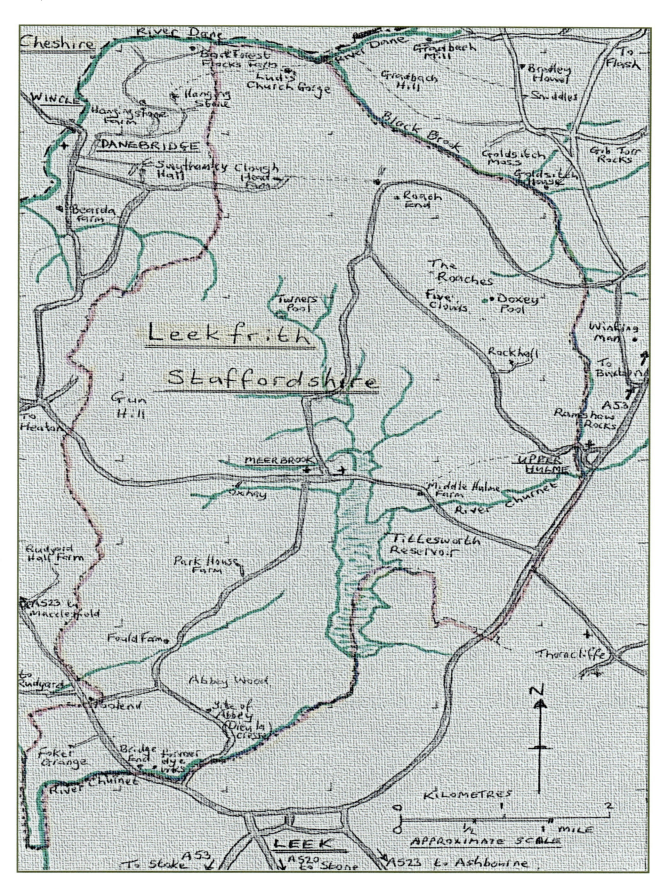

Map of Leekfrith Township

1.3 *Soay and Boreray - Rare Breeds of Sheep at Back Forest Flocks

The 'Soay' sheep breed descended from a breed which had its ancestry in domestic animals from the Mediterranean and Central Asia. The 'Soay' sheep were initially introduced from Europe, in the Iron Ages, when they became part of the descendant breeds placed on the Scottish Highlands and Western Isles, of which Soay was an almost inaccessible island with steep cliffs. The island of Soay is approximately forty miles from the Western Isles in an archipelago called St. Kilda, and it seems quite apt that the name of 'Soay' is an Old Norse word meaning 'Island of Sheep'.

The Soay breed of sheep is much smaller than the modern domesticated breeds but is much hardier as they have been allowed to become wild, or feral. Being very agile and sure footed, they tend to take refuge amongst cliffs when they feel threatened, so the island of Soay is probably their perfect habitat. They are classed as one of the short-tailed sheep breeds, coloured either black, or dark brown, but more recent breeds are often blonde or brown with a cream underbelly. A few have white markings on the face, generally with one pair of horns, but some have two pairs. They have been allowed to become feral in general, and this has benefitted the eco-systems where they have grazed, particularly because they can graze in places that other domesticated breeds cannot. However, they are few in number, and are listed as, 'at risk' - category 4, by the Rare Breeds Survival Trust as there are only between 900 and 1500 registered ewes.

The breed has been introduced in other areas around Britain, living wild on the Holy Isle of Arran, as well as small populations in the Cheddar Gorge area, and near Woburn. It was also placed on other islands in the St. Kilda's, namely Hirta, the biggest island there, and Boreray.

The island of 'Boreray' has given its name to another breed of feral sheep that is being maintained at Back Forest Flocks. It is known as the Boreray Blackface, or Hebridean Blackface, and is one of the rarest breeds of sheep in the United Kingdom. It is the only breed of sheep to be listed as, Category 1 – Critical, by the Rare Breeds Survival Trust, as there are fewer than 300 registered breeding females.

The Boreray sheep breed are one of the few surviving descendants of the Scottish Dunface sheep breed. These were originally domesticated sheep tended by the crofters throughout the Scottish Highlands and Islands. In the mid eighteenth century, the crofter's sheep were primarily similar to the domestic ancestors from the Mediterranean and Asia, with short coarse wool, and all having horns, sometimes two pairs. Generally, their fleeces are grey or cream, though some are slightly darker and similar to the Soay breed. Rough in quality, the wool they produce is used in creating tweed carpets. Both males and females have horns. There were about 1000 sheep on the island of Hirta, where most of the island crofters lived, and about 400 sheep on Boreray island.

In the late nineteenth century, the crofters of the Western Isles started to cross breed the feral sheep with the Scottish Blackface breed, which had by then virtually replaced the Dunface breed throughout Scotland. In the 1930's, both the inhabitants and the sheep from the island of Hirta were 'evacuated', and they were replaced with Soay sheep which were thought to be able to survive living as wild feral animals on the island. This was also the case for putting sheep on the islands of Soay and Boreray.

In the 1970's about half a dozen Boreray sheep were taken to the mainland to form the basis of a breeding population, but the majority of the Boreray sheep remained on the island, though only a small number compared to the Soay breed populations. It is remarkable, to me at least, to think that from a small handful of sheep taken from the island there is now a breeding group in such close proximity to us in Staffordshire. It must feel like a million miles away from their normal habitats, and I applaud the efforts of the Back Forest Flocks Farm to maintain the breed which is in danger of disappearing forever.

1.4 *Mills on the River Dane

There had been a corn mill at Danebridge in 1652, near to the bridge, and right next to the site used for the chapel that was built later. The corn mill was adapted so as to become a cotton mill in 1783, which was also used as a meeting place for Methodist followers from 1806, before they used the chapel that was built next to it in 1834.

Also, in 1652, near to Bearda farm, which is about a mile south of Danebridge, there was a paper mill. This was still in operation in 1742 but had closed down by 1754 when another mill at Whitelee became more favoured due to its new technology which incorporated a 'Hollander' system.

There was also a 'fulling mill' at Danebridge in 1671 which was operating up until 1715, but apparently closed down in 1742, and the location of the mill is unclear, though it may have been at the site where Folly Mill stood, as it had been rebuilt on a couple of occasions.

A 'fulling mill' was used for beating and cleaning cloth in water. The process shrank the loose fibres of the cloth, making it a denser fabric. To produce a superior cloth, it was usually 'fulled', dyed, brushed with teasels to raise the pile, and finally trimmed to remove loose threads to produce a finished surface of greater quality than the original cloth. Originally 'fullers' or walkers, trampled the cloth with their feet in a trough of water known as 'stocks'. The adoption of 'fulling' mills, sometimes known as walking mills from the 1300's, were in the process of being moved to heads of water sources in the countryside, as opposed to previously when they were generally located in towns. Greater quantities of superior cloths were processed more quickly as a result.

The lower quality cloths were placed into the 'fulling' stocks, along with some 'fuller's earth' (a form of 'soapy' clay), and then water was pumped in. The cloth was then pounded with wooden hammers, which were driven by a tappet wheel turned by a water wheel of the mill by the river, or brook, where the mill had been built next to.

The corn mill at Danebridge was adapted in 1783 to become a cotton mill, as mentioned above, by a John Routh, who was listed as a cotton manufacturer in Danebridge. There was also a John and James Berresford who were listed as cotton spinners at Danebridge in 1834. In 1841 there were nine cotton workers listed as living near the mill in the census. Only eight years later, in 1849, the cotton mill was closed, but it was re-opened in 1851 by John Bennett, a pattern designer, who was listed as living in the cotton mill at Danebridge.

The mill closed again in 1861 but was re-opened in the 1870's by John Birch, the owner of a dyeworks in nearby Froghall. He was also a carpet manufacturer in Wildboarclough on the Cheshire side of the Dane near Wincle. In 1876, his son Joseph Birch used the Danebridge mill to make colours for the silk trade, which was prospering with the nearby Macclesfield silk producers, only to fall into decline by the time of his death in 1898. There were then two mill buildings that stood next to the Methodist church in Danebridge, both were multi – storey buildings that fell into disrepair and were demolished in 1976.

Upstream on the River Dane from Danebridge, at Gradbach, another mill was rebuilt in 1785. This is still in place on the bank of the River Dane but has been converted into accommodation for nearby Newcastle under Lyme College. Possibly used as a cloth fulling mill initially, it was used to produce flax and then later used for silk production, before it was closed in 1868. It was later used as a saw mill at one point, before it was taken over by the Youth Hostel Association and finally bought by the college.

Gradbach Mill

In 1792, the land owner Sir Henry Harpur, the Lord of Alstonefield, gave out a 31 year lease to three businessmen in order to build, or rebuild what was a fire damaged mill on the bank of the River Dane at Gradbach. Thomas Oliver and James Oliver, of Longnor, and Thomas White of nearby Hartington, who were described as cotton dealers, soon had the mill up and running, only to be found bankrupt two years later.

Gradbach Mill was rebuilt during the reign of King George III (1760 – 1820), as above, after a fire damaged it in 1785. It was built at a time when the king was offering subsidies to stimulate the domestic production of flax and hemp, as there were currently expensive duty charges on imports of these products. The mill was built with the River Dane providing the power source to turn the machinery required to produce cloth in the mill. It is missing now, but originally on the side of the mill there was a huge waterwheel. It was recorded as being 38 feet in diameter, and with 96 buckets large enough to contain 35 gallons of water each. This would enable approximately 2,500 revolutions of machinery inside the mill to one complete cycle of the wheel outside.

In 1798, the lease for the mill was transferred to John and Peter Dakeyne, cotton spinners from Darley, in Derbyshire. They converted the mill to the production of flax and built a warehouse. By 1837, the mill had added another warehouse of three storeys, and also added a large house. The mill was providing employment for 64 people in 1838. The Dakeyne family were still operating the mill in 1850, now headed by Bowden Dakeyne, working with both flax and silk. The mill was still working although in decline by 1864, but it closed all operations down in 1868.

It was later used as a saw mill for local joinery woodwork before 1978. Then the mill, and mill house, were both bought by the Youth Hostel Association (YHA), who converted it for accommodation purposes. It was opened in 1984 as the Gradbach Youth Hostel. In the last two years, the building was sold to the College at Newcastle under Lyme to be used as an outdoor pursuits centre.

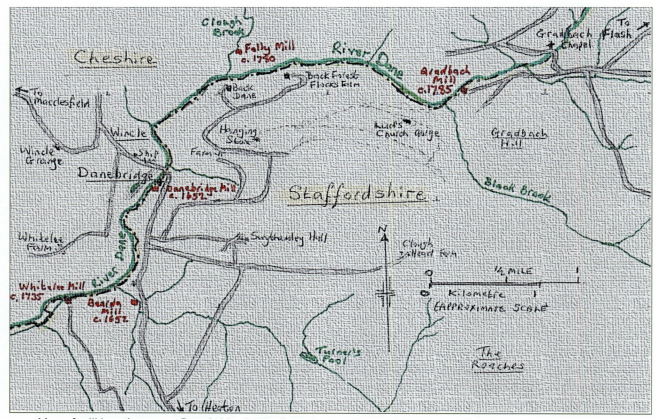

Map of mill locations near Danebridge in the River Dane valley, c. 1652 to c.1785.

1.5 *" LUD ' S CHURCH "

"Lud's Church" is a deep chasm that was created by a landslip on the hillside near to Gradbach and Danebridge. It is located in the wooded area known as Back Forest. It is approximately 100 metres in length, and about 18 metres deep. There are always damp conditions in the gorge, causing mosses and other vegetation to thrive, and the floor is constantly wet with muddy patches.

Lud's Church was formed, it is thought, probably after the ice age period, about 10,000 years ago. Its rock structures are mainly within a thick bed of coarse carboniferous sandstone, known as the 'Roaches Grit', which form part of the 'Goyt Syncline' in this area. The rocks in the area are traversed by numerous faults and fracture planes, and weak layers of mudstone exist within the sequence of rock layers. It was along these lines of weakness that a large mass of the 'Roaches Grit' slipped slightly downhill towards the Dane valley, resulting in the open rift.

The name of 'Lud's Church' has had various stories related to its chosen identity. In the early 15th century, the area was known to be frequented by the 'Lollards', who were followers of John Wycliffe, an early church reformer. They were rumoured to have used the hidden cleft as a secret place of worship. Lud's Church may have been named after Walter de Lud-Auk, who was captured here after one of their meetings.

Another story was that a wooden female figurehead, from a ship named 'Swythamley', stood in a high niche at the top of the chasm, placed there by Philip Brocklehurst, the then landowner, around 1862. The figurehead was called 'Lady Lud' and was supposed to have commemorated the death of the daughter of a Lollard preacher.

Various legends have also been attached to the chasm, including stories of famous people using it as a hiding place. These include Robin Hood and Bonny Prince Charlie. Another story tells of a horseman killed when out riding his horse, by the name of 'Lud', who was thrown into the chasm whilst chasing deer. He is said to have been seen as a ghostly figure, covered in muddy moss and leaves, giving rise to legends of 'the Green Man'.

Local 'Luddites' were known to be active in the area too, and they thought that Lud's Church was the location of the 'Green Chapel' as told in the story of 'Sir Gawain and the Green Knight', and it is not unrealistic to suggest that the word 'Lud' is an abbreviation of Luddite, and hence gave rise to the name of Lud's Church.

Sir Gawain and the Green Knight

A legendary story from the times of King Arthur was written by an unknown author, possibly 'Cameron of Sutherland', in the late 14th century. It is described as a 'Middle England' chivalric romance and is written in poetic stanzas of alliterative verse. The story is a portrayal of what was known as 'the beheading game', which typically involves a 'hero' character who goes on a quest to test his prowess. The Green Knight is interpreted by some as an allusion to Christ, and to others it is a parody of the folklore of the 'Green Man'.

The story describes Sir Gawain, who was a knight of King Arthur's 'Round Table', accepting a challenge from a mysterious 'Green Knight'. The quest was for any knight to strike him with an axe, as long as the deed was to be reciprocated in one year and a day in the knights own 'Green Chapel', which Sir Gawain had to find.

Gawain accepted the challenge, and duly beheaded the Green Knight with one blow. However, mysterious magical forces are said to be involved here, as the Green Knight nonchalantly picks up his head, and reminds Gawain to be at his Green Chapel in one year and one day.

Several stories have attempted to portray the quest of Sir Gawain in his journey to find the Green Chapel. The poem itself mentions the 'Islands of Anglesey', which today is just a single island. Gawain is said to pass the 'Holy Head', which is believed to be either Holywell, or the Abbey of Poulton in Pulford. Holywell is associated with the story of the beheading of Saint Winifred. Winifred was apparently a virgin who was killed because a local leader was refused his sexual advances towards her. Her uncle, who was a saint himself, put her head back in place and healed the wound, leaving only a white scar.

Gawain's journey leads him into the centre of the region where the author was thought to have originated. The dialect of the poet himself, who was dubbed the 'Pearl Poet', as he also wrote three religious poems in a similar way – 'Pearl', Purity', and 'Patience', is known as a 'North West Midland' dialect of Middle English.

The poem mentions the Castle at Hautdesert and the Green Chapel in the same area. Hautdesert is thought to be in the area of Swythamley, near Danebridge, as it lies in the poet's dialect area and matches geographical features described in the poem. The area was also known for the animals hunted, i.e. deer, fox, and boar, in the 14th century.

The Green Chapel was described in the poem as "two myle henne" from the old manor house at Swythamley Park, at the bottom of a valley ("bothm of the brem valay") on a hillside ("loke a littel on the launde, on thi lyfte honde") in an enormous fissure ("an olde caue, or a creuisse of an olde cragge").

Having seen the chasm myself, now known as Lud's Church, I can see this being the location of what is described in the poem. The green mossy vegetation that adorns the chasm is enough to see why it would be known as – The Green Chapel.

My first walk ends here with a somewhat tenuous link to the second walk, in that the story of Sir Gawain, a knight of King Arthur's Round Table, was obviously in the thoughts of the local pub landlord in nearby Flash. The 'Traveller's Rest' has a dual name that has been incorporated from the Lud's Church legends and takes your imagination into an old Middle England era by having the name of – The Knights Table – for its Medieval themed restaurant.

DISCOVERING STAFFORDSHIRE

An Historical Companion Guide

To Walking In North Staffordshire

Flash Village and Three Shire Heads

(Walk No. GM02 — April)

My original plans for this walk were changed a few times due to various factors, but the basic idea was to start by linking up my first walk from Gradbach, then walk up to Flash village. However, as I was driving to Gradbach and found that the route was almost via Flash village, I decided to start my walk at Flash Bar instead. This was prompted, although situated a few hundred metres north of Flash, by the fact it was here that the only source of refreshment in the area could be found, and it had a suitable parking facility.

As with my first walk, I had done some internet research in preparation for my route planning. I had a good idea of what I wanted to see, and what photos I wanted to take, but even some of that changed 'on route'. The first point of call was the Traveller's Rest / Knight's Table Inn, which is at Flash Bar, and has a large car park at the rear if required, though permission will be needed. This inn was known as the Traveller's Rest as far back as 1834, which is only a few years after it was thought to have been built, but I am not sure if it was given this name at the time of construction.

From there, heading down to Flash village on the busy main road, you can see to the right, what had previously been the highest hill in Staffordshire, namely Oliver Hill. The honour now goes to Cheeks Hill, which is about a mile further north, after some county boundary changes were made. On the left, as you walk back down the main A53 road, just below the Knight's Table, is the source of the River Manifold. From here the river flows down to meet the River Dove about 12 miles downstream, but this initial site is a little underwhelming I thought, as it resembles something like a small duck pond.

My route then took me into Flash village, with its substantiated claims to be the highest village in Britain no less, with St. Paul's church being the highest 'village' church, and The New Inn being the highest 'village' pub. A little further on there is a large house, with a large set of steps, which is a converted Wesleyan Methodist chapel. It all seemed very quiet and low key today, almost like being in a ghost town.

Into the countryside then from here, via the slopes of Oliver Hill, up and over Wolf Edge, getting views of the 'Winking Man' rocks that I had passed earlier on the main road from Leek, and onwards via Knotbury to the 'Three Shire Heads'. This is the meeting point of Staffordshire with Cheshire and Derbyshire, where an old packhorse bridge spans the River Dane.

My route plan then took me downriver, along the Dane's Staffordshire bank, to Knar farm, where my plans to get to Gradbach were changed. Due to poor footpath signs, or indeed a lack of footpath, I found my way along farm driveways away from the river, and onto a bridleway to a stream crossing, then onto a road back to Flash. Although this road would have taken me down to Gradbach if I had turned right, I decided to cut short my walk for the day and turned left, with a steep uphill climb all the way back to Flash. After my healthy, but almost exhausting, three hours of exercise, I then decided to take the drive home.

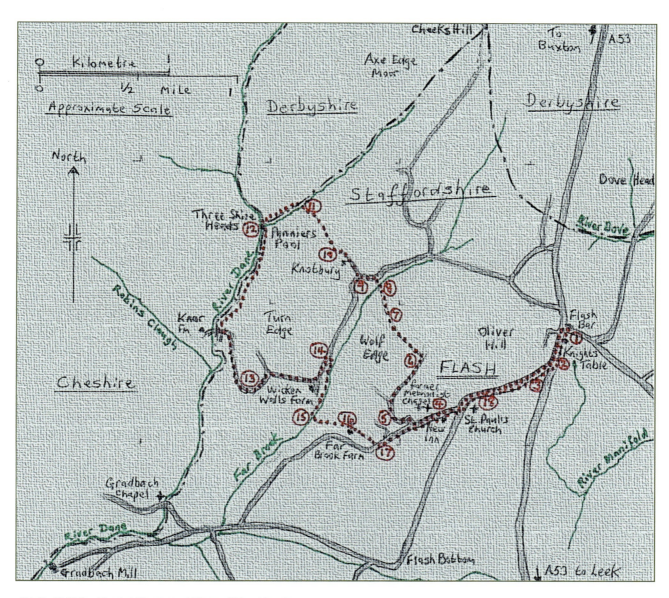

Walk GM02 - Flash Village and Three Shire Heads

38

Drive to the start point (Grid Ref. SK 03201 67863) using the A53 Leek to Buxton road. The famous landmark of the 'Winking Man' rock formation appears on your left, travelling from Leek, and continuing on you pass the sign for Flash village, which is a very tight left turn into a narrow road. Then about 200 metres further on, take a right turn at the bend for the Flash Bar shop/café and the Knights Table Inn (also known as the Travellers Rest). A car park is available at the rear of the inn, but it is necessary to get permission as it is for customers only. (Ref. for parking - contact – theknightstable@aim.com)

Walk details

Starting at Flash Bar, then into Flash village (England's highest village at 1518 feet), and on to Oliver Hill and Wolf Edge. Continuing then down to the Three Shire Heads, which is the meeting point of Staffordshire with Cheshire and Derbyshire at a river junction known as Panniers Pool. Then continue down the bank of the River Dane to Knar Farm. - Returning from there via Wicken Walls Farm and Far Brook Farm, which leads you to a steep uphill climb on the narrow road back to Flash Village. The whole walk takes about 3 hours, and is about 4 miles long.

1) - Start from the Knights Table Inn, as it is now called, which has a medieval themed interior and is the third highest pub in England. From the car park at the rear turn left and keep left back down the main road, the A53, where after about 100 metres on your left is the 'head' of the River Manifold, which appears to be a small duck pond. Further down the road you will need to cross the busy road to get to Brown Lane, which is the small narrow road on the right in to Flash village.

The Knights Table / Travellers Rest – at Flash Bar   (Picture kindly supplied by The Knights Table)

2) – The view of the head of the Manifold valley is not that inspiring here, but there are better sights along its 12 mile course before it joins the river Dove. Looking over the road you can also see the rising ground over Flash village. This is Oliver Hill, which was the highest point in Staffordshire at 1,683 feet until boundary changes meant that the honour went to Cheeks Hill a little further north, at 1,710 feet.

Head of the River Manifold, near Flash

View of Oliver Hill from Flash Bar (at 513 metres, or 1683 feet.)

3) - Walk along Brown Lane into Flash village, where you will see the welcome sign for Flash (Highest village in Britain, 1518 feet). Then there is the school on your left, until you come to St. Paul's Church, Quarnford parish, the highest church in Britain. The church standing today was built in 1901 as a replacement on the site of the original building that was erected in 1744.

Road into Flash village – Brown Lane

St. Paul's church, Flash village - (parish of Quarnford) – Highest church in Britain at 1518 feet

4) - At the church is a road junction, where left is New Road which heads down to 'Flash Bottom', but keeping right you will pass the New Inn pub. This is not much to look at, but this is actually the highest "village" pub in England, being at 1518 feet above sea level. Continue along this road, when you will see a large cube shaped building on your right, with steps up to the doorway. This was a former Methodist chapel, built in 1784, with Sunday services held here. It was rebuilt in 1821 for the Wesleyan Methodists, but it was closed down in 1974, and later converted into the house that is seen today.

Former Methodist chapel in Flash, as rebuilt in 1821

5) - Walking past this building, continue along to the end of the road where to the right here you will see a drive/track for Bank House. Another house here on the left sees a pathway going left behind the house. Go left taking the path behind the house to a gateway and stile. Keep left here down a clear driveway/track, with a view of Oliver Hill on your right, and soon you will see on your left the ridge known as Wolf Edge clearly in view.

6) - At the end of the pathway there is a metal gate which has to be climbed over as it is in need of repair at present. Continue down a well - trodden muddy path towards the rocks on top right of Wolf Edge. Climbing over a stile into a muddy patch of ground try to keep left of a small stream here. After about 200 metres you turn left at a gateway, and still heading for the rocks on Wolf Edge.

*(Time of walking here is approximately 30 minutes)

Rock outcrop at the top of Wolf Edge

7) - Continue heading uphill, veering slightly right to the top of the ridge, and just left of the rock outcrop on Wolf Edge. Turn around to get a nice view of the "Roaches", including a distant "Winking Man". At the top of the ridge now, keep the rocks on your right then head downhill on a grassy pathway until you come to some boggy ground and a stile. Keep the wire fence here on your right until you come to another stile about 75 metres further down. Keep heading down in what appears to be a dried stream bed, heading for the road you should be able to see at the bottom of the ridge.

8) - Near to the bottom, the path veers left towards the bend in the road and away from a wall. However, it does get a bit muddy here too, you should see a small stone footbridge over a stream to put you onto the road. Turn left onto the road and head for Knotbury.

9) - After about 100 metres, the road has a triangle junction, where you should take the right turn, even though there is a "T" junction sign. Walking slightly uphill, the buildings on the left being part of Knotbury Farm, you should spot a sign for "The Old Barn". Continue on the road up the hill, veer left at the bend where there is a 'narrow road' sign and passing another farm building which is 'Knotbury Lea Cottage'.

10) - Just past this building is a signpost on your left pointing across the field, but this has quite a few cows in it today, and luckily is not the footpath you need to take. Follow the road a little further down, which bends slightly to the right. You should see an older sign post pointing in a similar direction with the words on it reading as "Three Shire Heads". Go left here as directed by the post, slightly downhill to a gate. Then the pathway turns right and then descends on a slightly rocky path to another stile and a gate. There is a small bridge over a stream, with a signpost showing 'Orchard Common' to the right, but you need to go left here along the far bank of the stream, which is actually in Derbyshire.

*(Total walk time so far now is approximately 1 hour 15 mins.)

11) - Walk down the stream bank, which is on the Derbyshire side, until you come down to the River Dane and you see the old packhorse bridge, but also a smaller bridge over the stream you have been following that drops into a small pool area known as "Panniers Pool". This is the point where the "Three Shire Heads" meet, Derbyshire is to your right. Cheshire county lies over the packhorse bridge, and Staffordshire on the left bank of the Dane river. Our journey continues on the Staffordshire bank, which is part of the 'Dane Valley Way'.

"Panniers Pool" near the 'Three Shire Heads'.

View of the old packhorse bridge over the River Dane, and Panniers Pool

12) - The pathway goes uphill slightly with a sandy soil underfoot, and down to a metal gate, where the path forks. Take the right fork which goes down the bank of the Dane, which becomes muddy in places and with tree roots to negotiate. Continue down the path until you come to the river which has a wooden bridge over it into Cheshire. Keeping left, there is a driveway to a farm building, which is Knar farm. Although my map suggests a path beyond this farm driveway going towards Gradbach, I decided to go left here towards a barn building, slightly uphill. Then turning right, the path/track heads across a field full of sheep, as a driveway looking track up the hill.

13) - Follow the drive/track all the way to the end, with a hill (Turn Edge) to your left, when you come to a farm building. This is Wicken Walls Farm, where I came across a small area with chickens (keeping the pest problem under control).

14) – Continuing on, walk past the farmhouses, and through the metal gate, onto a small road. The road comes to a wide area where I think motor bike events take place. There is a steep hill to the left with trees where possibly some races take place. To the right is another farm house, keep to the road passing the driveway on your right, about 50 metres further on to your right you will see a signpost with a horseshoe sign (denoting a bridle path) on it pointing downhill towards the small stream at the bottom, which you may be able to hear trickling below.

15) - This is Far Brook, so head downhill on this narrow rocky and sandy path/bridleway, through a gate, until you come to a small footbridge which has a large sign by it denoting a public footpath, and by crossing the bridge you are heading back towards Flash village.

16) – The initial climb up the stream bank is slippery and muddy, but it levels out after climbing over a stile, which itself is quite a high obstacle. Continue on the grass pathway towards a pair of new looking wooden gates. These belong to the farm buildings here, Far Brook Farm, so continue through both gates, making sure you have closed both of them behind you, and head behind the buildings onto the driveway up to the main road that goes back to Flash.

17) – It is possible to take this road, by turning right here, all the way down to Gradbach. This is about a mile down the road should you feel you have the energy to revisit the mill and chapel as recalled from my first walk.

18) – Alternatively, as I did, I turn left and use all my energy to climb the steep roadway all the way back to Flash village, eating my previously unopened sandwiches on the way. I arrived back in Flash village, having taken a few breathers on the way.

*(Total walk time about 3 hours, by the time you get back to Flash Bar).

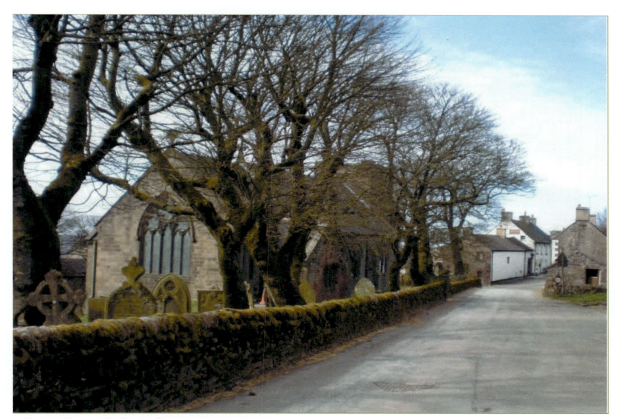

Flash village – St. Pauls Church and the New Inn.

2.1 Flash Village and Quarnford Township   - A Brief History

2.2 Coal Mining in Quarnford Township

2.3 Religion and Education in Quarnford

2.4 Methodist Movement   - and John Wesley

2.5 From Hugh le Despenser to Rushton Spencer

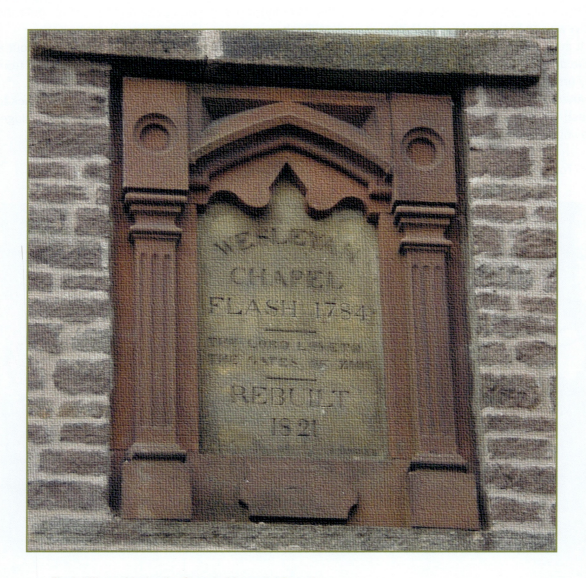

Flash Village Methodist Church 'Memorial Panel'

2.1 *Flash Village and Quarnford Township - A Brief History

Flash village is the main settlement in the 'civil parish' of 'Quarnford'. The name of 'Flash' is believed to be derived from a word meaning 'swamp', though as the area is the source of at least three rivers, namely the Dove, the Dane, and the Manifold, another definition that a 'flash' is also a rush of water may also be appropriate. However, the river sources do seem to spring from the water table reaching the surface in surrounding fields with more of a trickle than a rush, and some fields that I have walked in did give the impression of being in a swamp.

The name of Quarnford was recorded in 1227 and is thought to be derived from an old English word of 'cweorn', meaning millstone. The 'ford' part, usually referred to as a river crossing point, was possibly situated at Manor Farm near Gradbach. The name may also refer to a 'stopping place' on a route that was used to carry millstone, and in this instance, both the 'ford' and the stopping place may be 'Panniers Pool', at Three Shire Heads. Panniers, or a pair of large baskets, were used on horses and donkeys to transport millstone across the many trade paths in the area, and the 'stopping place' for drinking water for the animals may have been at the so called 'Panniers Pool'.

In the early 13th century, Quarnford was situated in the forest of Alstonefield Parish, which belonged to the Earl of Chester. A member of the Earl of Chester's household, known as 'Peter le Clerc', (later known as Peter the Clerk), created a 'park' for grazing purposes in Quarnford. Peter was succeeded by a Hugh Le Despenser, another member of the Earl's household, who erected a fence around the 'park'. The fence was taken down in 1227 to restore pasture rights. The park may have been situated near to Gradbach as there was an area there still called 'The Park' in 1630. In 1321, the parish was known as the 'Manor of Quarnford' and was under the ownership of Hugh Despenser (the Elder), whose grandfather had been the overseer of the 'park' in Quarnford, as mentioned. Hugh Despenser (the Elder) was given the title of Earl of Winchester in 1322 by King Edward II, but due to misgivings of greed and wrongdoings at the 'Royal Court' by his son, Hugh Despenser the Younger, he was hanged in 1326. His son, Despenser the Younger, was put on trial for being a traitor and a corrupt thief a year later and was subsequently mutilated to death by having many body parts cut off whilst being tied to a ladder.

In 1327, the Crown assigned Quarnford Manor to Sir Roger Swynnerton, as well as Despenser's share of Alstonefield, and his manor of Rushton Spencer, all of which had been obtained through corrupt manipulation. In the mid - 15th century, the manors of Quarnford and Rushton were acquired by John Savage, and later his descendant, Sir John Savage, passed on farms and waste ground at the end of the 16th century to John Harpur, who was given the title Lord of Alstonefield.

Farming in the area was known to develop when a dairy farm was recorded in 1308, possibly beside the River Dane where Birchen Booth Farm once stood, near to Knar Farm which is just over the Cheshire border. The name Booth is probably derived from the word 'both', which was a name used for a cowhouse or herdsman's shelter. In 1597, a Ralph Rudyard, (who was a descendant of another Ralph Rudyard, supposedly the slayer of King Richard III at Bosworth, and who had Rudyard village and lake named after him), held a lease for 300 sheep gates in Quarnford. By 1988, records show there were over 840 cattle and more than 6,900 sheep in the civil parish of Quarnford, and farming is the main source of employment in the area today.

Quarnford was formerly a 'township' in the parish of Alstonefield, which has the village of Alstonefield itself about 12 miles to the south–west of Flash. The township later became a civil parish. In 1751, the township recorded a population of 218 adults over the age of 16, and by 1831 there were 783 adults recorded. However, thereafter the numbers began to decline, mainly due to a loss of jobs in both the mill at Gradbach and in the local mines. The main source of occupation became agricultural work, of which there was a limited requirement. In 1931, there were only 296 people recorded in the township, and this went down to 222 in 1991, which is virtually the same number as it was some 240 years before.

Flash village had only five houses in 1597, and it grew slowly up to the time of the church being built in 1744. The church itself however was rebuilt after years of neglect in 1901, which is the church of St. Paul that stands in the village at the present time. In 1817, Flash village had three inns and three shops, and by 1904 a post office had been built. Today the shops have gone, and only the New Inn pub remains in the village, though the Travellers Rest/Knights Table at Flash Bar is technically in the village some 400 metres up on the main Leek to Buxton road.

In 1771, there was a tollgate built, which was called Flash Bar, and it still remains the name of the road junction now. There was a toll house at the crossing junction of the main road, which then ran from Leek to Buxton (which had been realigned itself in 1749), with a road that ran from Macclesfield, via the packhorse bridge at the Three Shire Heads, on to Longnor village. This tollgate was still in use up until 1852. There were also toll houses at a house now called Bradley Howel, and one near to Manor Farm at a house now called Greens.

At Flash Bar, an inn was built approximately 1824, and in 1834 it was recorded with the name of 'The Travellers Rest'. This was used as a meeting place for the local people, and in 1840 a club for the sick was based at the inn, called the 'Quarnford Club', which had been in existence since 1767. It was set up to collect money for the sick and for burials, as a benevolence fund society. In 1846, it was known as the 'Flash Loyal Union Sick Club', until 1906 when it was renamed the 'Tea Pot Club'. This was dissolved in 1991, but in a form of remembrance the local people of Flash have a service in the summer, followed by a parade called the 'Tea Pot Parade' when they march from Flash village, with a band accompaniment, carrying a tea–pot up to Flash Bar.

Flash had been known as a gathering place for 'hawkers', and other rough characters who would squat on open land, travelling from fair to fair selling wares. Many gatherings led to 'prize fights' being set up at the nearby Three Shire Heads, where the counties of Staffordshire, Cheshire and Derbyshire met at 'Panniers Pool'. During the time when Gradbach mill was producing silk and cotton, there was also a thriving cottage industry in Flash, and the surrounding settlements, making buttons with button presses. There were plenty of rumours spreading that a gang were using the presses to make forged coins, and there are records of forgers being hanged at Chester after a servant girl was caught giving out forged coins. This led to a name attachment of 'Flash Money' being used, and the theme of an alleged counterfeiting of bank notes in Flash was used in a novel, called "Flash", by Judge Alfred Ruegg in his 'historical romance' written in 1928.

2.2 *Coal Mining in Quarnford

Industry in the area may have started with the transport of millstone, but there is a record from 1401 of the first coal mine in the parish. A certain Thomas Smith took out a lease for one year for a 'vein' of coal at Black Brook, near Upper Hulme. This was the first of many coal mines, as it was followed by mines at Orchard Common, Black Clough, Hope, Goldsitch, and Knotbury. They were all worked throughout the 18th and 19th centuries.

As the pottery industry was in full swing in Staffordshire, there was a need for coal as a source of fuel to heat the kilns. The first coal workings in Quarnford began around 1400, and the surrounding area was being regularly searched for new outcrops of coal at the surface, which were usually found in streams. There were records of coal pits in the Goldsitch Moss area in the south of the township in 1564, and some workings of coal at Black Clough in the north in 1602.

Sir John Harpur, the Lord of Alstonefield and new owner of some of the land in Quarnford, gave a lease on a house, thought to be Goldsitch House, and its surrounding land to a Peter Higson. The lease included all coal works in the Quarnford township for 21 years, for which Mr. Higson had to pay an annual rent, of £12 and two fat hens !

Coal was also dug in 1673 along streams to the south and east of Orchard Farm, near Knotbury. In 1677, another lease was given by Sir John Harpur to a William Wardle. This was followed by the next generations of landowners when Sir Henry Harpur gave leases on coal mines at Goldsitch and Knotbury in 1765. Two men from Derbyshire, namely George Goodwin and John Wheeldon, and a third man – James Slack of Knotbury, were listed as the leaseholders. It is assumed that a James Slack had asked the two Derbyshire men to pay his lease costs for a cut in the profits. The lease was for £10 and 15 shillings a year, for 21 years, which would have been very expensive for a coal worker at that time.

In 1841, there was a record in the new census of 20 coal workers in the township of Quarnford, then 32 workers in 1851. However, by 1881 there were only 14 coal workers listed, as the main workings at Knotbury had closed down, and only used to provide for local demand. The last mine in the surrounding area was at Hope colliery, near Alstonefield - some 12 miles away from Flash, which was last worked between 1925 and 1932.

2.3 *Religion and Education, in Quarnford

Up until 1744, the people of Quarnford parish are thought to have travelled over ten miles to attend church at Longnor village. The journey must have been thought to be too excessive, as the land owner at the time, Sir Henry Harpur, decided to donate a plot of land in Flash village where a local church could be built. The original church was built by the local inhabitants of the parish, at the site where the new St. Paul's church (built in 1901) stands today.

The church of 1744 was of a simple construction, being a single room/cell building of brick, with stone dressings. A tower was added in 1750, with an external staircase on the west facing wall giving access to a gallery erected in the same year. In 1754, the church was extended eastwards, following a donation from a John Bourne of Newcastle-under-lyme who was a noted benefactor of churches in North Staffordshire. The eastern extension included a Venetian styled window. By 1830, although there were plans to rebuild the church entirely, there was an addition of a small vestry on the north-east corner, as well as additional east and south facing galleries. In 1857, a pulpit and reading desk were built on the internal north side of the nave. An organ had been acquired from St. John's church in Buxton in 1871, and in 1873 Lady Harpur Crewe had donated a font for baptisms.

The first curate of the church in 1744, a Daniel Turner, was to be paid £15. Of this, £10 was paid by 32 local inhabitants/landowners in return for an allotted pew in the church. The remaining £5 was paid by the trustees of the chapel, and there was a chapel warden in place in 1747. Daniel Turner was already the curate at nearby Meerbrook, and he later became curate at Rushton Spencer. He also lived at Meerbrook, where he died in 1789. Turner's successor as curate was a James Whitaker, who himself became vicar of Alstonefield in 1814. He employed 'stipendaries', people paid by the clergy, to serve Quarnford parish. One of these stipendiaries was Robert Balderson, whom the chapel warden had tried to oust from the church in 1821 because he was thought to be 'a most depraved and drunken man'. Later in 1821, the appointment of a James Roberts as the perpetual curate brought about an improvement in relationships with the warden.

James Roberts lived in a house in Flash that was rented from Sir George Crewe. By 1840 however, the house had become dilapidated, so much so that Roberts successor decided to live in Hollinsclough village, nearly five miles away. Successive curates of Quarnford parish continued to live in Hollinsclough until a vicarage house was built in Flash in 1884. This was no longer needed by 1963 and was sold as a private house.

By 1794, fifty years after it was built, the old church in Flash was in a very poor condition and plans were set up to completely rebuild it. However, that was still the intention in 1841 after the additions of the vestry and two galleries. The parishioners themselves could not afford the cost of rebuilding, and it was only in 1901 that the church was finally rebuilt, even though many more additions had been made. Known as the Anglican Church of St. Paul in Quarnford Parish, the church was built in its 'Gothic' style, to the designs of W.R. Bryden from Buxton. The pulpit of 1857 was replaced with a new stone carved pulpit, a donation from a local sculptor named Edward Ash. The original churchyard had been extended in 1857, and in 1898, then furthermore in 1927.

The noted church benefactor, John Bourne, had a school built in Flash in 1760. The building was apparently attached to the New Inn pub, and the chapel clerk was made the school master in 1764. In 1830, the township had a Sunday school that was attended by both Anglicans and Wesleyan Methodists. The school received £5 per year from a donation left in a will by a Laurence Heapy, who died in 1828, the curate of Macclesfield. The donation was intended for the religious education of all poor children who attended the church at Flash. Later in the 1830's there were two Sunday schools in Flash, one for the Anglicans and the other for the Methodists. In the 1851 census, records show the Church of England Sunday school was attended by 50 persons, and the attendance in the Wesleyan Methodist Sunday school on the same day recorded as 51 persons.

(Note : - although my religious knowledge is a little limited, it has struck me that there was a leaning towards the Methodist movement at this time, as reflected in the number of chapels I have already seen in just a few walks. I have done a little research into the Methodist movement, and John Wesley, and this can be found in the following section.)

Less than thirty years after the Anglican church was built in Flash in 1744, a house in Quarnford parish was registered for protestant dissenters by a local man named Thomas Redfern in 1772. The house was evidently used by Methodists, estimated to be attended by about 40 people. The meeting place was thought to have been in Flash village itself, as in 1784 a Methodist chapel was built in Flash. The Methodist society had 60 members listed in 1784, and more than 90 were listed six years later.

Sunday Methodist services were held on a fortnightly basis in 1798, and then weekly from 1802. As other Methodist societies were being established in neighbouring villages the size of the society in Flash began to diminish. It still remained the largest society in the area, and in 1821 the chapel was rebuilt as a Wesleyan Methodist chapel. By 1851, the attendance on census Sunday was 80 in the afternoon, and 180 in the evening. However, in 1974, the chapel was closed down and sold as a private house.

It may, or may not, have been a coincidence, but in 1772, Thomas Redfern was registering a house for protestant dissenters in Flash. That same year in Longnor village a private prayer meeting was held by John Wesley. This was attended by about 18 people, and I would not be surprised to find the name of Thomas Redfern in the list of persons attending. The importance of the name of John Wesley being in the area preaching the ideology of the Methodist movement would have been too good an opportunity to miss.

2.4 *Methodist Movement and John Wesley

"Methodist", became a widely used term in the 1700's to describe people who were very 'enthusiastic' about their religious beliefs. The earliest 'methodist' preaching in Britain took place in the 1730's in Wales, where the voices of Howell Harris and George Whitefield were heard spreading the gospel. Methodism was part of an international movement that stemmed from Germany in the 1600's with the 'Pietists', who were so called because of their disciplined piety, which was seen as a devotion to the belief in salvation through faith in Jesus. The movement was spread to Britain by the Moravians, who were originally from the Czech Republic, a Protestant sect with the view that the Bible was the only source of faith.

Perhaps the best known Methodist pioneer in Britain was John Wesley. He was born in 1703, the fifteenth child of Reverend Samuel Wesley and his wife Susanna Annesley. Samuel Wesley was an Anglican rector in Epworth, Lincolnshire, preaching the views of the Church of England. John Wesley was sent to be educated in London, at the Charterhouse School, and then went to Oxford University. He was ordained as an Anglican deacon in 1725 and became a priest in 1728 at Oxford's Christ Church Cathedral. He became a Fellow of Lincoln College (Oxford), where he joined a group of like - minded friends, including Howell Harris and George Whitefield, in what was called the 'Holy Club', whose disciplined beliefs were similar to the 'Pietists', but they were attributed with the name of 'Methodists' in an attempt of mockery to their faith.

John spent more than a decade of spiritual searching, including an unpleasant period of missionary work in America where he encountered the Moravians. He had travelled with his only brother, the younger Charles. Then, it is claimed that in May of 1738, John had a 'spiritual experience' that convinced him that the truth of salvation lay in the faith in Jesus Christ. He began to preach that this salvation was available to everyone. There was a major divide developing among the Methodist followers, with two groups forming known as Calvinists and Arminians. Calvinism tended to stress the power and authority of God over who could be saved, whereas the Wesleys, both John and Charles, chose to embrace the Arminian emphasis which gave the choice of each person to respond to God freely, with the opportunity for all to be saved, through faith in Jesus.

George Whitefield, who had been a fellow member of the Holy Club in Oxford, chose the Calvinist ideas in his preaching. In fact, he was chairman at a meeting of the first Methodist Association in 1742, held at Watford, near Caerphilly in Wales. The meeting was attended by William Williams of Pantycelyn, and Howell Harris, amongst many others, to discuss the organisation of societies in a move to promote Christianity in Wales. Perhaps this is why, even today, much of Welsh Methodism is greatly influenced by Calvinism. A few years earlier, George Whitefield had invited John Wesley to go to Bristol, at Hanham Mount, to start open air preaching. It was in Bristol that John built the first Methodist building, which he called 'our new room'. Nearby, also in Bristol, his brother Charles Wesley had a house built, and although Charles had become an Anglican priest, following his father's beliefs, he too had an experience of an evangelical conversion like his brother John, and became an influential Methodist preacher in his own right. He was to become a prolific hymn – writer, and was responsible for the words that became the famous carol, 'Hark ! The Herald – angels sing.'

John Wesley gave over fifty years of his life to preach the Gospel. He had travelled to London in 1739 to start preaching there in an old cannon factory, known as 'The Foundry'. Later, in 1778, he built a new London chapel, with two houses added to accommodate visiting preachers and one to live in himself. This was located at City Road, Islington, almost in the centre of London. He died in his house in City Road in March 1791 and is buried behind the chapel. Today there are approximately 500 chapels listed that are dedicated to the Methodist movement, with a further 100 or so historic Methodist sites. Not all of these are churches, as some are Georgian houses and worker's cottages, and some are outdoor preaching places. I am not sure how many of these sites I will discover in my adventures across Staffordshire, but I will endeavour to make a note of them in my walking accounts.

2.5 *From Hugh le Despenser to Rushton Spencer

As a link from this walk to the next, I found the story of the Despenser family most intriguing and worthy of a more detailed investigation. It was in 1227 when the name of 'Quarnford' was recorded for the area which was part of the forest of Alstonefield parish, and a park for grazing purposes was created by Peter the 'Clerk'. His name was originally Piers le Clerc, who was born in Malpas, Cheshire, and was a member of the household of Randle de Blundeville, the 6th Earl of Chester. Peter became secretary to the Earl, and was granted Thornton – le Moors, in Cheshire, for his services by the Earl. In some accounts, Peter is known as 'Piers le Clerc de Thornton', as he died in Thornton – le – Moors.

Peter was succeeded by the first in a line of Hugh le Despenser's, who in this first instance I will refer to as the 'grandfather'. Hugh, the 'grandfather', was also a recognised member of the household of the 6th Earl and was the person responsible for erecting a fence around Peter the Clerk's grazing 'park'. Later down the line, he had a grandson who was also called Hugh, and soon to be known as Hugh le Despenser the 'Elder'. He married Isabella, daughter of the 9th Earl of Warwick. They had a son in 1286, also named Hugh, and he was soon to be known as Hugh le Despenser the 'Younger'. His life proved to be very eventful, and not for all the right reasons.

Hugh the 'Younger' rose to prominence with his connections to the Earls of Chester, and Warwick, and became a royal chamberlain and a favourite of the King, Edward II. He became the knight of Hanley Castle, Worcestershire, and 'keeper' of the castle and town of Portchester near to Portsmouth. He was also the keeper of the Welsh town of Dryslwyn near to Carmarthen. He was knighted at the age of twenty in 1306, and in the same year he married Eleanor de Clare, daughter of the 9th Lord of Clare.

Hugh inherited the title of Lord of Glamorgan through his marriage, when Eleanor's brother Gilbert was killed at Bannockburn in 1314, and his title also gave him possession of Cardiff Castle. Eleanor was niece to the King, Edward II, and this connection put Hugh the Younger into the English royal court, where he used his charms to become a favourite of the King. He was granted Wallingford Castle by the King, which had previously been given to the Queen Isabella for life. This was the start of a troubled relationship between Hugh the 'Younger' and Queen Isabella.

As a courtier, Hugh the 'Younger' manoeuvred his way into the affections of King Edward II, and by 1320 his greedy character was taking hold by seizing the Welsh lands of his wife's inheritance, forcing the Countess of Lincoln to give up her land to him, and cheating his sister-in-law Elizabeth de Clare out of her lands at Gower and Usk. The barons at royal court soon voiced their displeasures to the king, who had little choice but to exile both Despenser the Younger, and his father, in August 1321.

Hugh the 'Elder' fled to Bordeaux in France, but his son, as audacious as ever, became a pirate in the English Channel, lying in wait to plunder British merchant ships. The barons who had forced the king to exile them proved to be no better, and quarrels over land ownership with the king caused the in house fighting to escalate, creating enemies amongst themselves. The king decided to bring the Despenser's back from exile the following year, in 1322, and made Despenser the 'Younger' his favourite once more. The king was glad to see him helping to despatch the unrest between the quarrelling barons, especially Lord Roger Mortimer and the Earl of Lancaster. The Despensers soon turned to their old ways, growing rich from their dealings in land administration and corruption, with the King turning a blind eye to it all.

It was Queen Isabella who started the downfall of the Despensers, who especially had a disliking for Hugh the 'Younger' after having Wallingford Castle taken from her. It was speculated that she had also been raped by Despenser the 'Younger', and that this was the main reason for her hatred. It also emerged that Hugh the Younger had tried to bribe French courtiers into assassinating the Queen because of her friendship with Lord Roger Mortimer. It would seem that Lord Mortimer's grandfather had apparently killed Hugh the Elder's father many years before, and revenge was on the agenda.

Queen Isabella and Lord Mortimer returned from France unharmed. In fact, they had returned with 1500 mercenaries in an effort to mount an invasion of England in October 1326. The King was taken captive and forced to abdicate his throne to his son, Edward III. Hugh Despenser the 'Elder' was found and hanged in Bristol on 27th October 1326. Hugh the 'Younger' was forced to go on trial for treason in Hereford, on the 24th November, which was really a formality from the beginning and he was duly sent for execution. The manner of his execution was a little blood thirsty though, as records suggest he was hanged first, but cut down before he had died only to be tied to a ladder so that his body parts could be cut off, and his insides cut out, before finally being beheaded and quartered.

DISCOVERING STAFFORDSHIRE

An Historical Companion Guide
To Walking In North Staffordshire

Rushton Spencer and Cloudside

(Walk No. GM03 – May)

The walk from Rushton Spencer to Cloud Chapel was originally going to be my first walk, before the Danebridge and Flash adventures. I was doing some initial research of the northern area of Staffordshire and I was immediately struck with the images that I came across of the 'Chapel in the Wilderness', the name given to St. Lawrence' church in Rushton Spencer. For various reasons, though somewhat unclear as to why, I decided to try the other walks before this.

The start point was always going to be at the Knot Inn, mainly because of the refreshment facility and the parking facilities. The planned route options all had St. Lawrence church at the top of my viewing list, and from there I could have chosen a variety of routes. In hindsight my route, across open fields from the church to get to the Bridestones, would have been better served by taking the road up to view Rushton Hall Farm, but I will plan that in a future walk.

Research into the Bridestones gave the impression that it seemed like a local mini version of Stonehenge, so I had to investigate this site, and my new found 'mission' to include as many churches, if not all churches, in my walks, meant that the next point of view had to be the nearby Cloud Methodist chapel. This was supposed to be followed by a strenuous climb up to the top of 'The Cloud' hill, but on the day I was a little tired so chose not to. I justified my decision by telling myself that the summit was actually in Cheshire, as the border with Staffordshire runs along the top ridge of the 'Cloud'. Apparently, the name comes from an old word of 'clud' meaning a rock, but I would say that this hill is a big rock.

Walking back from the Cloud chapel, I planned to take the road back down to Rushton on which I had driven a few times cutting through to Biddulph. I wanted to walk down this road in order to view a number of farm buildings, especially those that have been Grade 2 listed, as are other buildings in the area. With Woodhouse Green Farm, Peck's House Farm and Lee Farm possibly the pick of these to view.

There was a mill site lower down, next to a small stream that is a tributary to the River Dane, but this has been replaced with a splendid large house and made up for the lack of an old mill. Finally, there are the remains of the old railway line, which has now had the track removed and a wide public footpath remains. This is part of the 'Staffordshire Way' and goes back to Rushton where there is the old railway station, dated 1844, opposite the Knot Inn, though it has now been converted in to a house.

I finished here today, but this was only half of my intended walk. Originally, I was going to link up with a visit to Heaton hamlet, as this was noted as the name of the 'township' and parish. I wanted to see the Whitelee Mill weir site on the River Dane, down river from Danebridge, then walk back down the Dane riverbank to see more farms before finally getting back to Rushton again. Since I had been working this morning since 05:00 a.m., I decided to call it a day, and the second part of this walk has now become my next separate walk.

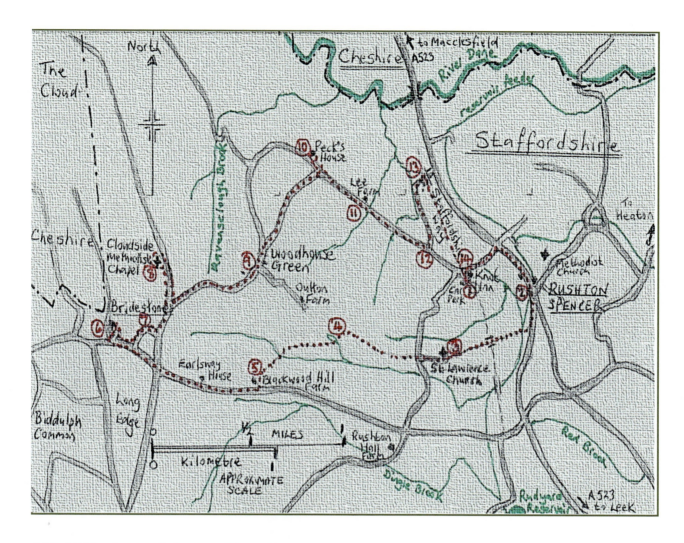

Walk GM03 – Rushton Spencer and Cloudside

<u>Walk Reference - GM03</u>   <u>Rushton Spencer to Cloud Chapel</u>

Drive to Rushton Spencer village using the A523 Macclesfield to Leek road. From either direction you will see the sign for 'The Knot Inn' on Station Road. Turn into Station Road where you will find The Knot Inn on your left after 100 metres. Turn into a driveway next to the pub car park, where there is a Staffordshire Council car park too. (Grid Ref. SJ 93625 62405).

Walk Details

Starting from the village of Rushton Spencer, heading for St.Lawrence' Church, known as 'the Chapel in the Wilderness', then across fields and along Beat Lane and Dial Lane to view the 'Bride Stones'. Heading back then, to see Cloud chapel, down to Woodhouse Green farms, Peck's House farm, and finally along a disused light railway line which is now part of 'The Staffordshire Way' back to the 'Knot Inn'.

The Knot Inn, Rushton Spencer

Old railway station – Rushton Spencer, building dated 1844, line opened 1849.

1) – Starting from the car park, walk back to Station Road, which is so called because on your left here, opposite the pub, is the old railway station house, dated 1844. This is the year the station building was built, but the railway line was not in use until 1849. I think the driveway to the council car park used to be where the railway line ran. Turn right for the main A523 road, and then turn right again along the main road. After about 250 metres you will come across Hammerton House on your right.

Hammerton House, on A523 Rushton Spencer

2)   – Just past here, with the Royal Oak pub over the road, there is a stile and footpath to your right. Climb over the stile and follow the grass footpath, then as it bends around you will see in the distance on the hill the first glimpse of 'The Chapel in the Wilderness'. Slightly muddy in places here, but you will reach a gate, which you go through and continue across the field rising towards a bridge. Go over the bridge, which has the Staffordshire Way underneath it going at right angles. You will see the church graveyard quite clearly now, and the last part is a little steep uphill climb to the gate.

Royal Oak , at Rushton Spencer

3)   – Various date plaques on St. Lawrence' church show that it has been built up over the centuries, with historical information suggesting that it was as early as 1386 when a bishop allowed a licence to hold services there. The board at the front entrance has a number of 1203, but that may not be a date, even so it is a nice old church. After viewing this, the exit to the main driveway is through another gate which has a small chain, but not locked. Be aware the field ahead had cows in it, which seemed friendly enough with me, so walk on slowly to the road. Opposite the driveway you should see a stile, over which are open fields. Climb over the stile, then this is where it got tricky, with no clear footpath to follow, you should either keep to the left of the field boundary or as I did walk directly across the middle.

- (Alternatively, you could turn left at the road (Bandridge Lane), walk about 400 metres up to a junction, then turn right, just before Rushton Hall farm, along Beat Lane to reach Blackwood Hill Farm, as noted below, hence missing out points 4 and 5).

St. Lawrence's Church, Rushton Spencer – "The Chapel in the Wilderness"

4)   – Heading across the field you should aim for the middle of two pylons in the distance. Also, there are two distinct trees, which are oak trees, where you will find a stile and an open gateway. Continue here into the next field and head for the pylons, then on the far side of this field you will find another stile, next to a round watering trough, with a public footpath sign which shows you are on the right track.

5)   – Over the stile, continue across the field heading for a brown/red coloured farm building, then through another open gateway into the next field heading for a whit gate. Just to the right of this there is a gap and a public footpath disc sign. Going through the gap, not taking the first left here as it is marked 'private', about 50 metres further on is a stile to your left. Another public footpath sign here, so climbing over the stile, negotiating wet and muddy area, walk between a hedge and fence, then a final stile brings you to a busy small road next to Blackwood Hill Farm.

*Walk time to here, approximately one hour.

6) - Turn right here along the roadside, be wary that Beat Lane is a busy road at times, walk up to Earlsway House Farm which is on your right after about half a mile, then about quarter of a mile further on to the left is the junction of Long Edge Road. Continue past this on to Dial Lane, when the road bends left with a junction on your right. Bear left past the junction, heading towards Congleton, then after about 150 metres you pass a large entrance to a house named The Bridestones. Just after this, turn into a tarmac drive to the right where you will find the site known as 'The Bridestones'.

The Bridestones , (off Dial Lane)

7) – Having viewed the stones, and perhaps taken a short lunch break, walk back to the main road, then turn left to go back up to a bend sign where there is a small road to your left. Turn left here into a small woodland triangular area, where the road then joins another small road. Go left here past Willowshaw Farm, then after about 200 metres take a left fork again where there is a signpost for 'Cloudside ½ mile', though my goal is only 200 metres away.

8) – As you walk down this small road, look to your left after about 200 metres where slightly behind a house and up a small walkway is the Cloud Methodist Chapel. Though dated 1815 on the building itself, preaching started on the site in 1811, and the local people built the chapel in three weeks in 1815. Plans had been drawn up in 1812, with names of Hugh Bourne, the preacher, James Bourne, the Harvey family and the Deakin family as principal directors of the plans, before it was finally built three years later.

Walk time now approximately 2 hours, (including viewing times).

(Note ; it was my original intention to continue past the church and make the climb up to the top of Cloud hill, but time got the better of me as well as energy).

Cloud Methodist Chapel, dated 1815

9) – You start heading back from here, by walking back towards the small junction and taking a left turn downhill towards Woodhouse Green. A nice stroll along this country lane, slightly downhill and uphill at times, brings you to one of what appears to be about three Woodhouse Green Farms, most of which are listed buildings. To your left you will get a good view of 'The Cloud', which you could walk up to if you have enough energy.

View of 'The Cloud' from Woodhouse Green Farms

10) – Continuing on here, there is a junction with a red telephone box, keep right with the sign for 'Rushton 1 ½ m' on a signpost, (note the other Woodhouse Green farms here which is slightly confusing), then carry on down for about half a mile to another junction. Look left here and you will see a large house and farm, this is Peck's House Farm, an old listed building, known to have been on this site since 1662.

Peck's House Farm, originally built c.1662

*Walk time now about 2 ½ hours.

11) - After viewing here, walk back to the junction, then continue down for a further 300 metres or so until you reach Lee Farm on the bend, built in the early 18th century, with an attached house that was built in 1793.

Lee Farm (early 18th century), and adjoining house c. 1793

12) - Further down the road you will come to another farm on your right, slightly elevated, which is High Lee Farm, and just a little further you will come to a road junction near to an old barn. Taking the left turn at the junction, the old mill house comes into view. A mill was recorded in Rushton Spencer as early as 1329, but I think this is a later house conversion.

House on site of old mill at Rushton Spencer

13) – Walking around the back of this house you will come to a small stream on the roadside, which I assume was used in the mill, though it seems tame now as it trickles slowly down towards the River Dane about 400 metres away. The stream continues straight on as the road bends round to the right under a bridge. An almost derelict house stands on the corner, and just by the bridge on the left-hand side is a set of wooden steps up to a wide footpath on the bridge. This is the now unused old railway line, converted into 'The Staffordshire Way' footpath.

14) - Follow this wide path all the way back to the Knot Inn, which is about half a mile away, where the walk comes to an end.

       *Total walk time – approximately 3 hours.

3.1 Rushton Spencer   - A Brief History

3.2 Chapel in the Wilderness

3.3 St. Lawrence , the Martyr   - The Holy Grail

3.4 Cloud Methodist Church and Hugh Bourne

3.5 The Bridestones

3.6 Rushton Station and the North Staffordshire Railway – Churnet Valley Line

The Bridestones

3.1 *RUSHTON SPENCER - A Brief History

In the Domesday Book, 'Rushton' was referred to as 'Riseton', yet the name Rushton is an Old English word that means 'a settlement by the rushes'. The 'rushes' were thought to be at an area of marshland in the valley to the east of the 'township' which became known as Rushton Marsh. The settlement took the suffix name of 'Spencer' following the 'administration' of Hugh le Despenser, who I have already outlined as a corrupt rogue.

Rushton Spencer was formerly a township in the parish of Leek, which was the largest parish in Staffordshire. The parish was divided into four administrations, namely Leek and Lowe, Bradnop, Endon, and Leekfrith. Leekfrith itself was sub-divided into a further six areas with Rushton Spencer being one, along with Rushton James, Tittesworth, Rudyard, Leekfrith, and finally Heaton.

Before the Norman Conquest, Rushton (or Riseton) was held by the then landowner Wulfgeat, who also had extensive lands in Cheshire. The land was taken by the King in 1086, who then passed the 'overlordship' of lands in the area to Ranulph, the Earl of Chester from 1129-1153, who in turn handed Rushton over to Norman de Verdun, of Alton. In the early 13th century his descendant Nicholas du Verdun had a daughter named Rose, who became the landowner of Rushton in 1242, along with Longsdon and half of Ipstones, but she unfortunately died in 1248, and the land was divided.

The northern part of Rushton became a separate 'manor', and just before 1326 when Hugh Le Despencer was hung, drawn and quartered, the manor became known as Rushton Spencer, leaving the du Verdun family with overlordship of only the southern parts, which became known as Rushton James. This was thought to be named after the du Verdun's land tenant, James de Audley.

Rushton Marsh was recognised in the mid-17th century as a separate hamlet in the township of Rushton Spencer, along the main Leek to Macclesfield road, where the oldest house was Hammerton House, which is still there today. In the later 18th century, a school was built on a side road headed for Heaton, and at the road junction of Sugar Street the Royal Oak Inn was built in 1818.

The medieval church of St. Lawrence became known in 1673 as the 'Chapel in the Wilderness', although it is thought to have been there for nearly three hundred years before. Its location as a solitary building, at least 400 metres from the settlements in Rushton Marsh and Rushton Spencer, and being surrounded by farmland today, giving rise to its 'nom de plume'.

Oulton Farm was thought to have been part of another small hamlet settlement in the Middle Ages, with the word Oulton being derived from the old English words 'ald' and 'tun', meaning an old farmstead. The nearby hamlet of Woodhouse Green was known in 1413, when it was mentioned as 'tenements of Wodehouse', perhaps even incorporating Oulton farm as a tenement.

The highest point in the township of Rushton Spencer is known as 'The Cloud'. The name is derived from the Old English word of 'clud', which means a 'rock'. The summit is approximately 1,126 feet (343 metres) above sea level, and the land then descends down into the River Dane valley at Hug Bridge, which lies at 390 feet above sea level only two kilometres away. Most of the western boundary of the township area of Rushton Spencer runs along the ridge from the Cloud summit to a monolith which was called the 'Stepmother Stone' and a mound which was called 'Mystylowe' in the 17th century. Mystylowe was the name used for the Neolithic chambered tomb now known as the 'Bridestones'.

In between the Cloud summit and the River Dane there is Peck's House, situated on the road from Woodhouse Green to Rushton Spencer, which was built around 1662. Lee Farm, which is a little further down the road, has Lee House next to it built in 1793. A mill was recorded in Rushton Spencer from 1329, which probably stood on the site of a water mill which was, in 1775, on the east side of the township. A mill was powered there by electricity in the 1950's, but then the mill pond was filled in when the mill closed down.

In 1848, the name of the inn at the bottom of the Woodhouse Green road was known as the Hope and Anchor. This was renamed in 1853 as the Railway Inn, as it was located next to the new railway station that was built in 1849. The inn was then renamed in 1991 as the Knot Inn, after the emblem of the Staffordshire knot, as used by the armed forces in the area.

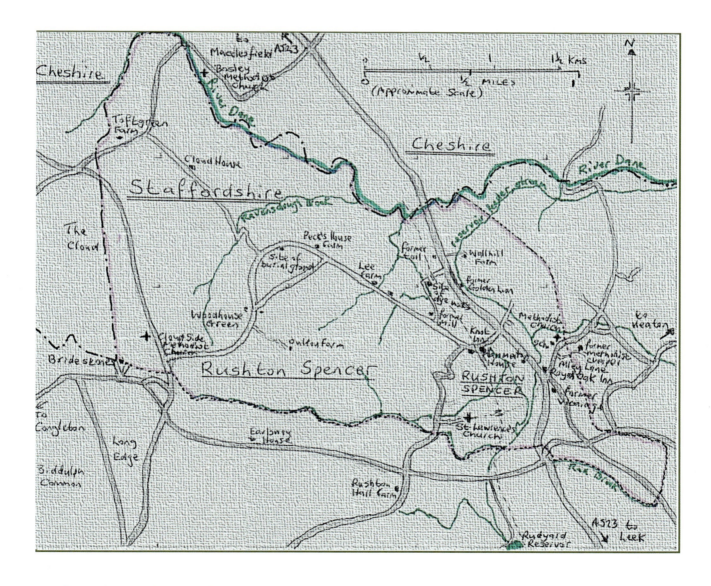

Township area of Rushton Spencer

68

3.2 *"Chapel In The Wilderness"

The 'Chapel in the Wilderness' is the pen name for the Church of St. Lawrence in Rushton Spencer. A church was allowed to be erected in Rushton Spencer after 1368 when the bishop for the parish of Leek gave a license to the inhabitants to have services in their own township. It was thought that it may have been built by the monks from nearby Dieulacres Abbey, but there is no documentation to verify this. Its remote location, surrounded by farmland, gave rise to it being known as the 'Chapel in the Wilderness', and it may have been built initially as a 'chapelry' (a district that is normally served by an Anglican chapel, though not recognised as a parish) in which the working monks could stop to say their 'offices' (daily prayers).

The chapel was still dependant on the parish church at Leek, despite having claims to 'parochial' status by the late 17th century. It was not until 1865 that the chapelry became a 'parish', after the inhabitants of Rushton Spencer attempted to have the chapel declared independent, so as to free themselves from having to pay fees as contributions to the repair bills of Leek parish church.

The chapel itself is built around a timber frame dating from the 14th century, which is within the outer stone walls that are largely of sand stone, and obviously from a later period. A date of 1690 can be seen above an east facing window, and a date of 1713 above the south doorway. The whole construction of timber and stone additions, especially the wooden roofing sections, probably make this a unique place of worship. There is also a short wooden tower, and an 18th century belfry. The nave and chancel have timber walls inside the building.

In 1830, and again in 1841, the Archdeacon of Stafford recommended that the chapel should be demolished and replaced with a new building, but, on both occasions, it was decided to repair the chapel instead. In 1842, some dormer windows were set in the south roof, and buttresses were built against the east wall for support.

The church was listed as a grade 2 building structure on the 1st February 1967, and other structures in the churchyard are also listed, including some memorials, a 'Chest Tomb', a 'Cross', a 'Headstone' and a 'Sundial'.

There is a grave for a 'Thomas Meakin', who was buried in 1781, which is the only grave that faces east. There is a mysterious story in relation to this which is of interest. Apparently, Thomas Meakin worked as a 'horse groom' and was in love with his master's daughter. His master was an apothecary, who did not approve of his servant trying to charm his daughter. However, Thomas suddenly died, and was buried hurriedly in the village of Stone, many miles away. Thomas's favourite pony however, who must have attended the burial, kept on running off to the grave in Stone and continually pawed the ground. The grave was exhumed, and the body of Thomas Meakin was found lying face down. This gave rise to rumours that he had been poisoned by the apothecary and buried alive. His family brought his remains back to be re-buried in Rushton at St. Lawrence's chapel, and had his grave facing east so as to have him remembered.

3.3 *St. Lawrence - The Martyr, and the Holy Grail

The name of St. Lawrence gave me an intriguing story when I discovered he was made a martyr and has a link to the mystery of the Holy Grail.

St. Lawrence is thought to have been born in southern Spain, in the town of Huesca. Lawrence grew up in southern Spain where he met the future Pope, Sixtus II. Sixtus, who was Greek, had become one of the most famous and highly esteemed teachers in Zaragoza. Both men became friends and soon left for Rome, where Sixtus became the Pope in AD 257. He ordained Lawrence as a deacon and was appointed first among the seven deacons who served in the patriarchal church. Lawrence was therefore known as an archdeacon of Rome, and as such warranted a position of great trust that included the care of the treasury and riches of the Church, as well as being responsible for distribution of 'alms' to the poor.

A year later however, at the beginning of August AD 258, the then Roman Emperor, Valerian, issued an order that all bishops, priests and deacons should be put to death along with the Pope himself. Valerian had decided that he would denounce all Christians, and, being a greedy pagan, decreed that they would all be executed and all their goods and belongings would be confiscated by the Imperial Treasury. It was thought that the Church had a great fortune hidden away and the deacons were ordered to bring all the treasures they had to the Emperor.

Sixtus was captured on the 6th August and was taken for execution. As he was led away, Lawrence called out to him saying, "Where are you going without your deacon". Sixtus replied, "I am not leaving you my son, and in three days you will follow me". Sixtus was then taken to be beheaded by the Emperor's soldiers. Lawrence was then told to bring the treasures of the Church but said that he would bring them to the Emperor in three days time. In the next three days he went around the city of Rome gathering together all the sick and poor people that were supported by the Church, and took them to the Emperor saying, "This is the treasure of the Church".

Valerian was disappointed with Lawrence and condemned him to a slow and cruel death. He was tied to a metal iron grid and placed over a fire that slowly roasted Lawrence's flesh, but as Lawrence was slowly dying he supposedly called out and cynically said, "Turn me over, I am done on this side". Lawrence prayed that the city of Rome would be converted to Jesus, and that the Catholic faith might spread all over the world. Soon he had succumbed to his fate, and is thought to have uttered, "It's cooked enough now", just before he died. It was August 10th AD 258, and is now known as St.Lawrence's Feast Day.

There is some speculation as to whether he can be considered as a martyr, and a letter 'p' is to blame apparently. Ancient records from the time of his death show the words 'assus est', which is translated to mean 'he was roasted'. This has been misread over time to be 'passus est', which is the phrase for 'he suffered and was martyred'. Pope Sixtus II was recorded as a martyr for being beheaded during the same persecution, but there is some doubt to the martyrdom of St. Lawrence even now.

There is also a story of St. Lawrence, amongst many, that suggest miracles are connected in his name, with a tale that he was able to spirit away the Chalice used during Christ's Last Supper. The Holy Grail in one account, was thought to have been taken to Huesca, in Spain, where Lawrence's parents lived. There was a letter, and an inventory, according to Catholic tradition, sent with the Holy Grail by St. Lawrence to his parents. Lawrence entrusted the sacred chalice to a friend who he knew would travel back to Huesca, where it was to be taken to the monastery of San Juan de la Perla.

Whilst the exact journey of the 'grail' throughout the centuries is much disputed, it is accepted by many Catholics that it was Lawrence's parents who sent the grail to the monastery for preservation and 'veneration'. The term 'veneration' is used to describe an act of great respect and reverence, and today the Holy Grail is venerated in a special chapel in the Catholic Cathedral of Valencia, in Spain.

3.4 *Cloud Methodist Church and Hugh Bourne

Hugh Bourne (1772 -1852) was a joint founder of 'Primitive Methodism', which was the largest offshoot of Wesleyan Methodism. He was an influential voice in the Protestant Christian movement. Hugh was born on 03rd April 1772 at Ford Hayes Farm, in Bucknall, Stoke on Trent. After training as a carpenter, he moved to the nearby village of Bemersley, near Biddulph, and was apprenticed to his uncle as a wheelwright. Hugh specialised in making and repairing wheels for windmills and watermills.

He was raised in a religious family and developed a morbid fear of being condemned to Hell. He once said, "I have spent twenty sorrowful years in pursuit of salvation". His mother, Ellen, gave him an anthology of Christian writings in 1799, and after reading this he later wrote, 'I believed in my heart, grace descended and Jesus Christ manifested himself unto me, my sins were taken away in an instant, and I was filled with all joy and peace in believing'.

In 1811, he preached open air at Cloudside, not more than 200 metres from the 'Bridestones'. His preaching reputedly inspired the local people so much that they were determined to build their own chapel in response. They had collected enough funds, supposedly in three days, and set about building the chapel, which was built in three weeks, but only opened four years later in 1815.

Today, the chapel retains preaching plans dating back to 1812, showing the names of James and Hugh Bourne. The 'Primitive Methodist Chapel', as it was then, had an extension built in brick in 1958, and has been known as the Cloud Methodist church since 1991.

Inside the Cloud Methodist Church

3.5 *The 'Bridestones'

The 'Bridestones', or what remains of them, were placed, or 'built', in the Neolithic Stone Age as a burial chamber or cairn. The original construction site is thought to have been approximately 110 metres by 11 metres, but all that remains today covers a small area about 6 metres by 3 metres. The stones are located on the Staffordshire border with Cheshire, near to the 'Cloud' hill, at about 820 feet above sea level, just off the roadside between Rushton Spencer and Biddulph.

Evidence from a variety of sources suggest that the original structure was once a chambered tomb, with a paved forecourt in the shape of a crescent, with a large holed stone that divided the main chamber from the forecourt. The stones that remain today are thought to be from the main chamber, but there are reports from the 18th century, when most of it was still intact, that there were another two chambers, but no traces of these have been found in recent years. The remaining chamber consists mainly of two portal stone slabs, placed vertically with a height of approximately eight to ten feet. There is also a broken cross slab amongst some smaller stones in the 6 x 3 metres site.

The cairn, or chamber, had originally had four portal stones, with a stone circle surrounding it. From 1764 however, the site was ransacked for its stones, which were to be used to build a nearby turnpike road and a farmhouse. In 1766, there was an account written by Henry Rowlands, for the 'Mona Antiqua Restaurata', about the condition of the site of 'The Bridestones', part of which stated –

"There are six upright free stones, from three to six feet broad, of various heights and shapes, fixed about six feet from each other in a semi – circular form, and two more within, where the earth is very black, mixed with ashes and oak charcoal. It is apprehended the circle was originally complete, and twenty seven feet in diameter, for there is the appearance of holes where stones have been, and also of two single stones, one standing east of the circle at about five or six yards distance, and the other at the same distance from that".

This account seems to give the impression that there were more stones remaining than there are today. Especially as many stones were used for the turnpike road, and some were taken to make an ornamental garden in nearby Tunstall Park. From 1764, it is estimated that about a thousand tons of stone have been taken from the 'Bridestones' site. To add insult to injury, there are stories of a bonfire causing some stones to be cracked and broken in two, and an engineer from the Manchester Ship Canal using one of the biggest monoliths as a test piece for the purpose of carrying out a demonstration with a detonator. This may be the same monolith referred to by Henry Rowlands when he added –

"The sides of the 'cave', if I may so call it, were composed of two unhewn stones about 18 feet in length, six in height, and fourteen inches thick at the medium. Each of them is now broken in two".

The site is now protected as a 'Scheduled Ancient Monument' but is still accessible to view. In my view this so called protection has come about 150 years too late. Before the large scale ransacking of the site it appears that the 'Bridestones' were an incredible monument, and it is such a shame in that it should have been our local 'Stonehenge', as important to Staffordshire as the pottery industry.

A few thoughts as to the origins of the name, given as 'The Bridestones', have been suggested. One story suggests that a recently married couple were murdered at the site, and the stones were laid around their grave – but considering the stones are thought to be Neolithic I find this theory a little unconvincing, especially as no bones have been discovered. Another story suggests they were originally called 'The Briddes Stones', from an old English word 'briddes' meaning 'birds'. As the stones in their original form could have resembled bird shapes I found this a more plausible theory.

3.6 *Rushton Station and the North Staffordshire Railway - Churnet Valley Line

Rushton railway station, serving the village of Rushton Spencer, was opened in 1849, as part of the Churnet Valley Line and North Staffordshire Railway (NSR). The NSR was formed in 1845 when three individual companies attempting to gain Parliament backing for constructing new railways decided to amalgamate. The Staffordshire Potteries Railway, the Trent Valley Railway, and the Churnet Valley Railway thus merged, and launched a Share Issue through Parliament on 30th April 1845 to fund the construction of a linking railway network to the numerous towns and villages of North Staffordshire. The Churnet Valley Line proposed linking Macclesfield, via Leek to Uttoxeter, with new stations at North Rode, Bosley, Rushton, Rudyard Lake, and Rudyard between Macclesfield and Leek.

On the 26th June 1846, the NSR Acts of Parliament were passed, giving permission to start construction of three connected line networks. The tender for construction of the Churnet Valley Line was given to J & S Tredwell, and they began construction in September 1847. A section between Uttoxeter and Froghall involved closing a part of the Caldon canal and laying track in the canal bed. This was made possible as the NSR had just acquired the Trent and Mersey Canal company. Stretching from Uttoxeter, through Alton, and Leek, to North Rode where the line meets the main track to Macclesfield, there were several new handsome station buildings built along the route. The designs of A.W.Pagin were used at the stations of Froghall, Cheddleton and Rushton.

The lines carried the vast majority of china and other pottery goods in England, and also carried coal and other minerals. Passenger services were mainly local, though main line connections could be made at Stoke for journeys to Manchester or London. The NSR remained independent until 1923 when it became part of the LMS, the London Midland Scottish railway.

When the NSR took ownership of the Trent and Mersey Canal company in 1847, it made the NSR the biggest canal owning railway company, with 130 miles of waterways. They also had ownership now of nearby Rudyard Lake, which the NSR wanted to use as a leisure complex by building a golf course and a series of three hotels to promote tourism. The 'North Stafford Hotel' was opposite the Stoke on Trent railway station, the 'Churnet Valley Hotel' in Leek, and the 'Hotel Rudyard' at Rudyard station at the south end of the Rudyard Lake. The NSR finally overcame legal proceedings regarding the land ownership near to Rudyard in 1905. Thus, the golf course, boat hire and a dance floor, could be built to promote tourism in the area.

In 1923, all of Britain's regional railways were grouped into four major companies. The NSR became part of the LMS, which was not popular with local people, who feared their local railway service would suffer with cutbacks or closure. However, Alton Towers re-opened in 1924, having been closed since 1901, and this saw the steady increase in use of the new LMS line, with dozens of trains taking hundreds of visitors to Alton Towers.

The NSR had struggled to promote their own 'jewel in the crown' at Rudyard Lake (from which Rudyard Kipling gained his name). The lake was actually a reservoir that supplied water for the Trent and Mersey canal company, which was fed from a feeder stream from the River Dane, starting from a few miles north at Whitelee weir (which coincidentally forms part of my next walk). The biggest change that the LMS made was to sell the NSR's golf club and hotel at Rudyard Lake. The two stations were renamed on 1st April 1926, with 'Rudyard Lake' station named as 'Cliffe Park', and 'Rudyard' station being renamed confusingly as 'Rudyard Lake', was this some sort of April Fool's joke I wonder. Cliffe Park station became unmanned in September 1936, with the new Rudyard Lake station being promoted to encourage visitors to the attractions built there previously.

The railway line at Rushton Spencer remained in use until passenger services were withdrawn from the section between North Rode and Leek in 1960. Freight services continued until 1964, when the track was then lifted. The remaining track bed now forms part of the public footpath system, the 'Staffordshire Way'.

The final part of my walk here has been a small part of the Staffordshire Way, and this makes one link to the next walk, which is really the second half of a larger walk if you wanted to join them up. From a tributary stream of the River Dane, the old railway track bed takes you back to Rushton station where this walk ends and the next walk begins. The final part of the next walk also links back to the feeder stream for Rudyard Lake, which flows from the River Dane at Whitelee Weir. Whitelee also had a mill which is seen in a part of the section 'Mills on the Dane' mentioned in my first walk.

DISCOVERING STAFFORDSHIRE

An Historical Companion Guide

To Walking In North Staffordshire

Rushton Spencer to Whitelee Weir

(Walk No. GM04 – June)

Most of the initial planning for this section of the walk had been done with my previous Rushton Spencer area planning. This, in effect, is part two of the Rushton Spencer walk, as this walk's start point is exactly the same as the finish point and start point of my previous walk. The general plan was to see the Methodist church in Sugar Street, then make my way up to Heaton 'hamlet', across field paths to see the site of Whitelee Mill and the weir. Then walk down the south bank of the River Dane, where the feeder stream for the Rudyard reservoir lake runs parallel and then make my way back to Rushton Spencer.

Starting at the Knot Inn again, I followed the old railway line track pathway to the bridge where you can view the Chapel in the Wilderness and then I cut across a field walked previously to get to the Royal Oak inn. A view of the old vicarage house across the junction there and then what should have been a walk up across the field to Alley Way turned into a walk around the field and back to the Royal Oak, because the exit to the field had been fenced off.

Rushton Methodist church seemed a little too modern and left me wondering whether it had been rebuilt since the foundation stone dates of 1898. The next section was a pleasant walk across more fields to get to Heaton, where a brief visit to Heaton Hall farm trying to confirm whether or not it was the centre of administration for the 'township' of Heaton was a little inconclusive. A short walk up the road brought me to Heaton hamlet, which is a pleasant little triangle arrangement of quaint houses.

The track from there leads to Heatonlow farm and subsequent research informed me that I had missed a site of an old Anglo-Saxon cross about 400 metres along, in a field to the right of the track. It wasn't signposted so I am unsure to its exact location, maybe you will find it if you follow my walk route. The track/driveway leads to two buildings and in between them, heading right behind the first building, there is a gateway into fields which is where I lost my way a little. There is no definite clear pathway, so I had to follow my nose a little and hope I would regain my bearings. A few footpath signs did appear at the far fence to the fields but these were not that helpful in pointing me in the right direction either. I managed to scramble over a stream, and up a steep bank to climb over another fence, then into another field, before I managed to get a sense of direction at Hollin Hall farm. The occupants were luckily standing in their doorway and gave me directions to Whitelee weir, across another field.

Still, the trip was worthwhile when I eventually found the river and the impressive weir. The site of the old mill is not recognisable, but the start of the feeder stream for the Rudyard reservoir is picturesque in its own way. A small bridge across the river leads to a pathway to Danebridge if you should wish to revisit, but I turned around to find the pathway down the river leading to Barleigh Ford bridge. Along the way I passed a house being renovated, which had the name 'Feeder Cottage'. I later found this was a cottage where a bailiff lived who was employed to keep the feeder stream clear of debris and silt, although unfortunately this is not a job done today as the stream is pretty stagnant in many places.

A brief look at the Barleigh Ford bridge was a little underwhelming, then a slow trek along the Gritstone Trail along the side of the reservoir feeder stream brought me to the Rushton Inn on the main Macclesfield to Leek road. This last section may appear to be uninteresting, but a little research into the historical links in the area made it more intriguing. The stories of the feeder stream, the building of the nearby Rudyard Lake, the name of Rudyard, and other connections to Heaton township concerning land ownership all made interesting reading to me. However, I will leave you to judge that for yourselves.

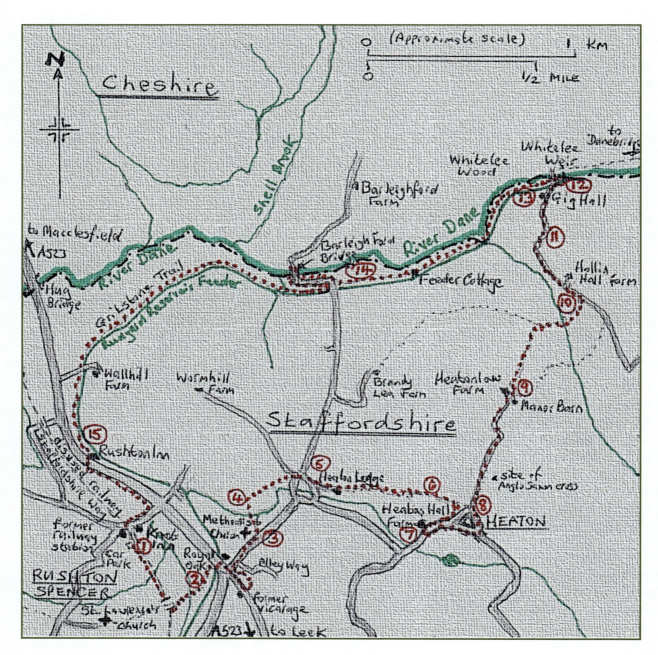

Walk GM04 – Rushton Spencer to Whitelee Weir

Walk Reference - GM04   Rushton Spencer to Whitelee Weir

As with the previous walk, I drove to Rushton Spencer village to park on the council car park next to the Knot inn. (Grid Ref. SJ 93625 62405). Having got to know the country lanes a lot better now, I used a route from Stoke via Biddulph, past Biddulph Grange House, which is also well worth a visit. (In fact, my wife and I have been there this past month and walking around there gives a little inspiration if you like your gardening). The narrow lanes from Biddulph Grange rise uphill, past a farm that keeps llamas with a plastic zebra in the field? Turn right at the crossroads via Dial Lane, then near to the Cloud Methodist chapel and the 'Bridestones', as noted in the previous walk, turn left down into Rushton to the Knot Inn.

Walk Details

Starting from the council car park in Rushton Spencer, continue on to the Staffordshire Way, which is now a disused railway line pathway, towards the 'Chapel in the Wilderness'. A previously walked pathway to the Royal Oak pub, then up to see the Rushton Methodist Church. A trek over fields on some hard to find walkways, (actually, most are non-existent), then on to Heaton Hall farm and Heaton village. A walk along a track/drive to Heatonlow farm, is followed by another trek across fields, and then across a stream. This is where I got a bit lost but eventually found my way to the best part of the walk at Whitelee Weir on the River Dane. A steady walk back to Rushton along the Dane bank, and then alongside the Rudyard reservoir 'feeder' stream which runs directly back to Rushton.

The walk takes about 3 ½ hours, though I did make a few wrong turns and doubled back on one section and is about four miles of fairly easy walking terrain, apart from a muddy stream bank.

1) – Using the council car park as the starting point, go right past the barrier onto the Staffordshire Way footpath, which is a wide disused railway track now in light woodland. After approximately 250 metres you can see St. Lawrence's church, or the 'chapel in the wilderness', on the hill to your right. Then there is an old stone bridge, which just under, and on the left, is a small path up to the bridge top. Left here takes you up to the church, which was part of the last walk. So, from here, we go right across the field heading for the Royal Oak pub on the main road, dodging the cows as you go.

Cows sunbathing in the field near the Royal Oak

2) - Cross over the busy main road, heading right at the Royal Oak, where there is the junction of Leek Old Road and Sugar Street. On the right-hand side of Leek Old Road is the 'Old Vicarage' house, which is a pleasant building. There is a public footpath post on the left-hand side of the road, just opposite the old vicarage house, but when I climbed the two stiles and ducked under some tape that the owners of 'Redway House' have put in place, then climbed uphill to the opposite side of the field, I found no possible exit to Alley Way, when the map book suggests there should be. So, I had to come back down to the junction at Sugar Street to make my way to the next viewing point, the Rushton Methodist church.

The 'Old Vicarage' house at Rushton Spencer

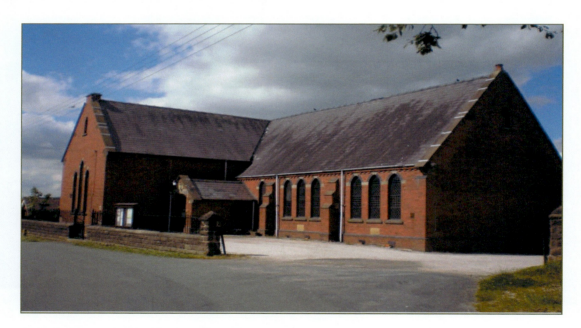

Rushton Methodist Church – on Sugar Street

3) - Walking up Sugar Street, go past Alley Way on your right, where I had originally intended to walk down from. The primary school is on your left, and then just around the bend is the modern looking Rushton Methodist Church. The beige foundation stones near the base of the building are dated 31st May 1898, one with 'laid by' Mrs. S. Goodfellow, and the other is 'laid by' Miss Lucy Anne Torr.

*(Walk time, so far, including lost time in field at Redway House, about 40 minutes).

4) - Just past the church, on the left-hand side of the road, is a narrow entrance for a public footpath between hedges. Along this path is a metal gateway, followed by a downhill path with boarded steps. A large flat wooden bridge spans a small stream into an open grass clearing that has been mown recently, and you can see a gated fence with a 'Private' sign. Just to the right of this gate there is a stile, and a Countryside Care marker pointing in the direction of a large field. Another stile into the field, which then has an uphill walk until you see another stile next to a missing gate for the next field ahead. Walk across this field, then after another stile, into the next field which has sheep grazing, then on your right you should see a stream. Keep near to the stream, heading for the farmhouse in view ahead. In the corner of the field, near the farmhouse, there is a stile to climb over, putting you onto a small track and road junction.

5) - Turn slightly right but then go straight over the crossroads, along the road/track with a wooden fence on your right. As the road forks, keep left where you will see a public footpath sign pointing up the driveway to 'Heaton Lodge Farm'. Walking up to the farm you will see another public footpath sign pointing to a stile, and steps on your right. Light woodland at the side of the farm buildings has a path that takes you past the farm, with a slight uphill walk towards a largish tree. At the tree I turn around to see a view of 'Cloud Hill' behind the farm, and generally nice views all around here.

Heaton Lodge Farm, with 'The Cloud' in the distance

6) - Under the tree here, there are some stone steps into the next field. Keep to the right where you should be able to hear the trickle of a stream, and with no clear footpath you should head for the farm ahead. A gateway puts you onto a small concrete road that goes slightly left and uphill. About 50 metres up, on the right-hand side is a small wobbly stile into the field. Head for the corner where you see a telephone power point with two tall posts. Unfortunately, I cannot see a way out of the field except by jumping over a small stone wall onto the road beyond it.

*(Walk time here, approximately 1 hour and 15 minutes).

7) - After negotiating the wall, turning right here I walk down the road to see that the farm there is 'Heaton Hall Farm'. There is a large house here too, which maybe I thought was the original Heaton Hall, and centre of administration for Heaton 'township'. Further investigations may be necessary to confirm this however. So, I walk back up the hill where the road goes to the centre of Heaton hamlet, and there are just a handful of houses. The road comes to a triangular junction, then at a road fork to the left, past Black Horse Cottage, there is a 'T' junction road sign and a public footpath post pointing down the track.

Heaton Hall Farmhouse

8) - Walk down the track marked with the 'T' junction for at least half a mile, (note: somewhere to the right here is an old Anglo-Saxon cross in the field, according to some later research), until an entrance to the grounds of 'Manor Barn' and 'Heatonlow Farm' are reached. Keep walking through the driveway area, where behind the building on the right is a large wooden gate. Go through the gate, making sure it is closed behind you as you enter a field full of sheep, and one spotted pig. Go left after closing the gate, and walk across the field, heading for what looks like a pointed hill on the horizon, (which may be Shutlingsloe Hill near Wildboarclough village in Cheshire). There is not a clear pathway to follow here.

9) - Keep walking past some small trees, and a heap of old straw, until you reach the far side of this large field where you should see a metal gate. However, this is padlocked, and walking right from here about 50 metres there is a small stile to exit into the field. The ground drops down to a stream under some trees, which is where I thought I could see a crossing point. Unfortunately, there is a wire fence, that has been climbed many times looking at its down trodden state, which I too crossed to get to the stream. With no proper pathway, jumping the small stream was easy enough, but a steep muddy bank the other side would be very difficult to climb up in wet conditions. I think there must be an easier route if I had gone downstream a little, but I persevere through woodland up to the top of the bank where there is another stiff wire fence before a field. I search for a stile along the fence, but I must have gone in the wrong direction again by going upstream. Finally, I find a gap but it is not the right path, but I am in the field and I can see a metal gateway on the other side with a small road, so that is the point to aim for.

*- (Walking time now, approximately 2 hours).

10) - Turn left onto the concrete road, then after about 100 metres you will see on your right another stile and a public footpath sign which is where I should have come out after crossing the stream, so that tells me that the route I took was not the marked map route. Just past here you will see the driveway entrance to a building, which has a cattle grid. This is 'Hollin Hall' farm, where another track forks to the right going to the barns. By walking carefully over the cattle grid there is a sign for Gig Hall. (Note; gained direction from the residents of Hollin Hall to the weir, which regained my bearings, so many thanks).

Hollin Hall Farm

11) - Just past the sign for Gig Hall, there is a hard to see Staffordshire Council marker on your left, which points to another stile on your right. Climbing over this stile puts you into a field, with an almost recognisable pathway across it towards a stile on the opposite side of the field, next to a tree. Make your way to this stile, and then cross over into a small marshy area with a pathway that leads downhill, and the sound of running water can be heard. This is the River Dane, and at first I thought I was hearing a waterfall, then as I descend some boarded steps down the steep bank the impressive sight of the Whitelee Weir comes into view.

12) - There is a foot bridge over the river here by the weir, and a footpath signpost on the Cheshire bank which leads to Wincle and Danebridge villages upstream. On the Staffordshire side you can explore the remains of what used to be the raceway for Whitelee Mill, which is now demolished, and there is a 'feeder' stream for Rudyard reservoir running from there, parallel to the river. In between the river Dane and the feeder stream there is a clear pathway, which is marked as the 'Dane Valley Way'(DVW), some parts of which we have seen before on my previous walks.

Whitelee Weir on the River Dane

Whitelee Weir and a bridge to the Danebridge footpath

Whitelee Mill site workings, obviously overgrown, and the feeder stream for Rudyard Lake

13) - Just by the footbridge, on the Staffordshire bank, there is the start of the footpath, with a sign for Barleigh Ford Bridge. Start walking down the pathway and a few minutes along there is a building on the right with a sign on it which reads, 'Feeder Cottage'. This was a derelict building back in 1992 and is being transformed into a nice house. It was once a bailiff's house who was employed to maintain the feeder stream, keeping it free of debris, so as to keep the flow going into Rudyard Lake.

Feeder Cottage, near Whitelee Weir and River Dane

14) - The pathway continues with a couple of wooden gates and stiles to negotiate, and near to a stone bridge over the feeder stream there is a track that goes, downhill and slightly right, down to the River Dane, where you will find Barleigh Ford Bridge. The track continues on into Cheshire, and the bridge is fairly ordinary, so after a quick view of the river I make my way back to the stone bridge on the feeder stream. Just to the right-hand side is a footpath, with a sign for 'The Gritstone Trail', which continues the journey along the feeder stream. The feeder stream is now quite overgrown with reeds and other plants in places, as well as the odd fallen tree, and this makes this part of the walk a little disappointing at times, as the neglect of the waterway takes away what may have been a more pleasant scenic route in the past.

View of the River Dane at Barleigh Ford bridge

*(Walk time now, approximately 3 hours and 10 minutes).

15) - The Gritstone Trail starts with a wooden 'clapper' gate, and from there it goes on for about a mile, with a few stiles and farm driveways to cross, and after a few more gates, it reaches the main road that you can see, and hear, up ahead. The trail reaches the side of a building, which is 'The Rushton Inn', where a broken fence enables you to get on the footpath of the main road. The trail does continue a little further behind the inn, but it had lost its scenic quality a long time ago, so I cross the main road and head back to Station Road, where we started at the Knot Inn.

Rushton Inn, on the main Leek to Macclesfield road A523

*- (Total walk time back at the car park, approximately 3 ½ hours).

HISTORICAL COMPANION GUIDE TOPICS   -   WALK GM04

4.1   Heaton Manor and Township   - A Brief History

4.2   Anabaptists and Methodists in Heaton Township

4.3   River Dane   - Feeder Stream - Rudyard Reservoir

4.4   Whitelee Mill and Folly Mill   - Hollander system

4.5   James Brindley   - Millwright, wheelwright, canal engineer

4.6   The Brocklehurst Baronetcy and the Shackleton Expedition

4.7   Brocklehurst's Wallabies   - the Roaches and the Winking Man

Feeder Cottage, near Whitelee Weir

4.1 *HEATON MANOR AND TOWNSHIP - A Brief History

A _'tithing'_ was the name given to a group of ten households, which were considered for the paying of tithe tax in a system of 'frankpledge'.

A _'tithe'_ was a rural land division, originally regarded as a tenth of a 'hundred', which is a name given for an administrative district of land.

A _'frankpledge'_ was an Anglo–Saxon legal system in which the unit of ten households, or tithing, were collectively responsible for each other's conduct. In effect, each member of ten households was regarded as a responsible member of a community that had a corporate responsibility to effect the good behaviour of each other. It was really a self-policing system aimed at keeping good behaviour in the community.

A _'headborough'_ was the name given to the chief member of a frankpledge, who was ultimately responsible for the whole group of ten households. A 'headborough' was normally appointed by a court of the manor.

A _'grange'_ was classified as a farm, or a country house with farm buildings, belonging to a monastery or a feudal lord of the manor.

A _'manor'_ was a tract of land granted with rights of inheritance by a royal charter.

The manor of Heaton was included in a grant made by Ranulph, the Earl of Chester, in 1232. The grant was made to pass the overlordship of Leek manor to Dieulacres Abbey. By the early 14th century, Heaton was made a 'tithing' of Leek manor.

Dieulacres Abbey had two 'granges' by 1291, with Fairborough in the south of Heaton parish, and Swythamley to the north, and the abbey recorded in 1535 that it held the 'manor' of Heaton. However, shortly after the 'Dissolution' (1536 – 1541), the Crown sold the Fairborough grange estate in 1546 to a William Fynney, who passed it down his family descendants until 1618 when it was sold to George Thorley of Heaton. The Crown retained the Swythamley manor until 1614, when it was then divided and sold in two transactions to a William Tunnicliffe, of Bearda Farm, and a William Plant, from Heaton hamlet. Together they sold the manor of Swythamley to George Thorley in 1629, who already owned the Fairborough estate. In 1631, the Swythamley estate was sold again and bought by a Francis Gibson, of Wormhough Farm, which lies in the west of the manor, and he then sold the estate, which was divided again, in 1654 into two transactions, one to a William Nabs, and the other to a William Trafford.

During the 1640's, the Fairborough grange estate was occupied by a John Pott, and his descendants held the estate until 1757, when part of the estate was sold to the Earl of Macclesfield. The entire Fairborough estate was broken up in 1919.

William Trafford and his family descendants held the Swythamley estate until 1832, when they sold what was then called Swythamley Hall to a John Brocklehurst, of Prestbury, Macclesfield. John was succeeded in 1839 by his son William, who unfortunately died without leaving an heir in 1859. The estate was passed on to his nephew, Philip Lancaster Brocklehurst (1827 – 1904). He was created a baronet in 1903, but died a year later, leaving his son Philip Lee Brocklehurst (1887 – 1975) as the successor to the estate and the baronetcy. In 1975, the baronetcy passed to John Ogilvy Brocklehurst (1926 – 1981), who was Philip Lee Brocklehurst' sister's grandson, and originally named John van Haeften. He broke up the Swythamley estate in 1977 when the hall and its parkland was bought by an Indian mystic group called 'The World Government for the Age of Enlightenment'. This was led by Maharishi Mahesh Yogi and was opened as a training centre for 'teachers of Transcendental Meditation'. In 1987, the hall was then sold to a Mr. R. M. Naylor, who divided the main house and outbuildings into a number of separate private residential units.

Heaton 'manor' was to become a township and a civil parish. The 'township' area that it covered, being one of Leek parish' nineteen townships, stretched from the River Dane in the north, starting near Back Forest Flocks farm and through Danebridge village, then along the river down towards Rushton at Hug Bridge. The 'hamlet' of Heaton lies in the south west of the township, but the centre of administration for the township is unclear. It may have been at Heaton Hall farm, near to the hamlet, or at either of the previously mentioned granges, Fairborough or Swythamley.

Only ten people were recorded in Heaton manor in 1327 as being assessed for tax purposes, and by 1666 that number had only risen to 42. The population rose slowly to 179 adults by 1751 and reached its pinnacle of 430 inhabitants in the census of 1841. The population started to decline again thereafter, and by 1991 it was down to 274.

Heaton Hall Farm, was so called by 1851, at the site which was recorded as occupied from 1775, and then the buildings were almost totally rebuilt in the 1860's. About half a mile south from there is Heaton House Farm, which has a date stone of 1824, though this too was apparently rebuilt in the 1840's for a surgeon by the name of John Robins, who was recorded as living there in the 1851 census.

The earliest settlements in the township were thought to be at the sites of Wormhough Farm, and Wormhill Farm, to the west, in an area that was known in the late 1240's as 'Wurnuldealth'. Wormhill Farm is thought to have replaced a building called 'The New House' that was recorded there in 1702. In the early 16th century, there were houses recorded on the sites now called Heaton Low and Hollin Hall Farm. Heaton Low has a porch which has a date stone of 1651, and the initials of William Nabs, who bought part of the Swythamley estate in 1654 with William Trafford.

Hollin Hall Farm was largely rebuilt in 1896, and nearby, on the River Dane, was Whitelee Mill which was rebuilt around 1735 - 1742. This stood near to a property called Gig Hall, which was on the Staffordshire side of the river. The name 'gig' is significant, as Whitelee Mill was thought to have originally been a 'gig mill', another name for a 'fulling mill', which produced cloth. The fulling mill was closed down in 1742, and presumably was redesigned to become a paper mill in the same year, when millwright Abraham Bennett was commissioned to build a paper mill. He attempted to bring in new technology in the form of the 'Hollander' system and was greatly helped by his more well-known apprentice James Brindley. Unfortunately, Bennett died later that year in 1742, but the plans of the mill appear to show use of the new 'engine paper mill system' that incorporated the 'Hollander'.

On the Staffordshire side of the river, near to where the mill used to stand, there is the start of a 'feeder' stream from the river Dane, which was constructed around 1811. This feeder stream was dug out and channelled alongside the river, until it veers away from the river towards Rushton Spencer near to Barleigh Ford Bridge. This bridge over the River Dane was built in 1752, before which there was a ford recorded there in 1611. Approximately ten feet across, perhaps maybe more in places, the feeder stream continues past the Rushton Inn and the Royal Oak Inn. It continues through the hamlet of Ryecroft Gate where it joins up with Dingle Brook just before it runs into its eventual destination, some five kilometres away from the River Dane, the Rudyard Reservoir Lake.

4.2 *Anabaptists and Methodists - (Non-conformist religious followings) - in Heaton parish

In 1665, Thomas Goodfellow and William Goodfellow were recorded in Leek parish as two followers of the 'Anabaptist' movement. This was a radical Protestant movement that began in 16th century Europe, and had the view that baptism was to be used solely as an external sign of a believer's conscious acceptance of faith. In this, it could only see adults as being suitable for baptism as an infant would not truly be capable of showing an acceptance of the faith. They also advocated, the separation of the Church from any state involvement, as well as generally practicing a simple living standard and shunning all non - believers.

The Goodfellow family lived at Wall Hill Farm, which lies between Hug Bridge and Rushton Inn to the south west of the township of Heaton. Thomas Goodfellow registered a meeting place in Rushton Spencer township for Protestant worship, which was thought to be at a farmhouse on the east side of the hamlet of Woodhouse Green, where Anabaptist followers held services from the late 17th century. In 1688 there was an Anabaptist burial ground to the north east of Woodhouse Green, which was last used in 1780. Anabaptists continued to hold occasional services at one of the farm buildings of Woodhouse Green Farms until 1828.

Methodist services had been held fortnightly on Sundays in Rushton 'township' since 1798, then a Wesleyan Methodist chapel was opened in 1816 in Alley Lane, just off Sugar Street in Heaton township. By 1829 services were held there every Sunday, and at the Sunday service of the 1851 census there was an afternoon attendance, besides Sunday school children, of 86 people.

The chapel was closed down when it was replaced in 1899 with a larger brick-built chapel on Sugar Street, no more than 250 metres away. There are two foundation stones laid at the base of the building, one of which has the name of a Mrs. S. Goodfellow, who may well have been related to the Goodfellow family of Anabaptists mentioned above. The date on the stone is 31st May 1898, which is when building was started on the new chapel. The other foundation stone bears the name of Miss Lucy Anne Torr, who from the census of 1891 appears to have been born in 1888 and would have only been ten years old when the chapel was being built. Her father was a Joseph Torr, a farmer and shoemaker from Horton parish, and his wife, ten years older than Joseph, was named Ann and from Wincle parish. They lived at Pitt Slacks Farm in Rushton Spencer parish, whereas Mrs. Goodfellow, wife of Samuel Goodfellow, lived at Intakes Farm in Heaton parish.

From 1821, there had been another Wesleyan Methodist congregation that met at a place called Diglake Sunday school, which was also near the Leek to Macclesfield road. Services held there on the census Sunday of 1851 were attended by 50 adults in the afternoon, and about 80 in the evening. As the service at the Alley Lane chapel was at the same time, the two Methodist chapel attendances total about 166 followers of what were considered non - conformist religious views, amounting to nearly a third of the local area population. This is compounded by the attendance at Danebridge Methodist chapel on census Sunday of 1851, where 120 people attended the evening service. There was also a Primitive Methodist chapel built on the east side of the township in 1864, which was closed in the late 1960's. It was converted into a private residence in 1985 called Gun End House.

4.3 *River Dane – Feeder Stream – Rudyard Lake Reservoir

Rudyard Lake Reservoir was constructed by the Trent and Mersey Canal Company to provide water to the locks of the Caldon canal near Leek. Construction of a dam was started in 1797, with a John Rennie, a Scottish civil engineer, as consultant. The dam and reservoir were completed three years later, and a branch canal from the Caldon canal to Leek was completed in 1801 with a feeder stream from the reservoir at Rudyard providing the water supply to the canal system.

The village of Rudyard, just south of the lake, was apparently named after a Ralph Rudyard, who was a local man with the disputed reputation of being the person to have killed King Richard III at the Battle of Bosworth Field. It was recorded by a Jean Molinet, a Burgundian chronicler, that it was a 'Welshman' who had actually struck several blows to the head with a halberd to fell the king, who had lost his helmet in the final skirmish that took place on 22nd August 1485.

Initially, the reservoir lake was filled by nearby springs, but these proved to be insufficient at keeping the reservoir up to required levels. It was decided that a feeder stream would be built from the River Dane, a few miles north of the lake, where a weir had been built in 1809 at the site of what used to be Whitelee mill. A channel was dug from the weir, about ten to twelve feet wide, which runs for about four kilometres through Rushton Spencer village to reach the top of the reservoir where it joins up with Dingle Brook.

In 1823, the weir at Whitelee had to be rebuilt, and lowered, in order to increase the water supply to the lake, which was being drained a lot more due to extensions to the canal system requiring ever more increasing amounts of water. The Canal Company had to employ a full-time feeder bailiff, whose primary job was to keep the feeder channel clear of obstructions, such as fallen trees and vegetation, and also clear any build-up of silt deposits so as to maintain a steady flow of water from the Dane to the reservoir. A house was built near the weir, now known as 'Feeder Cottage', and it was reported that the bailiff, and his wife and family, provided refreshments to passing walkers and tourists. Having been there myself on this walk, I don't recall being offered a cup of tea and sandwiches as I walked by.

In 1846, the North Staffordshire Railway Company had taken over the Trent and Mersey Canal Company, and the lake was acquired in the process, as well as much of the land around it. A railway system was built connecting Uttoxeter to Manchester on the Churnet Valley Line, and because of the accessibility of new railway stations there was a steady flow of tourists and daytrippers to the Rudyard Reservoir. One of these visitors was John Lockwood Kipling, who was with his partner Alice Macdonald, on a daytrip from nearby Burslem in 1863. They enjoyed the place so much that they were supposedly inspired to name their first son after the lake, the now famous author 'Rudyard Kipling', who was born in Bombay, India in 1865.

The feeder stream today is almost completely silted up, and many fallen trees and overgrown vegetation make it look more like a stagnant canal than a flowing stream. This leaves the surrounding streams and springs as the only source of water supply to the lake, but this apparently is sufficient to supply the canal system beyond, under the normal circumstances of usage today. The reservoir has lost a considerable amount of water capacity due to silt deposits, and in the early 1900's there was a part time dredger on the lake which removed the silt. This was stopped, and apparently due to Health and Safety issues is no longer a possible option.

However, it is said that the canal system is as busy now as it was at the height of the Industrial Revolution in the 1850's, but these days its use is largely for pleasure trips, and not goods barges. With the system now being run by the Canal and River Trust, which was created as a charitable trust following the demise of the government–owned British Waterways, the plight of the feeder stream will be determined by income from donations, grants, and government money. Unfortunately, it would appear that other projects have more priority than returning this feeder stream to its former state.

4.4 *Whitelee Mill and Folly Mill - and New Technology on the River Dane

Wincle village, on the Cheshire side of the River Dane, was known in 1291 as a settlement called 'Wynkehull', or 'Wineca's Hill'. The crossing over the River Dane, known as Scliderford, being recorded in 1190, suggests that the settlement of Wincle had developed with the trade pathway, 'The Hollow Way', at about the same time that Danebridge village was evolving. Goods were regularly passing by on their way to markets in Macclesfield, especially wool which was traded by monks from Dieu La Cresse abbey near Leek.

Wincle had a 'grange' which was constructed from around 1400 AD by the monks from Combermere, near Nantwich, probably with the help of monks from Dieu La Cresse. It is thought that the grange had a watermill, and evidence gained from much later shows there was an agreement made between the monks of Dieu La Cresse and the monks of Crokenden. This was involving a mill near Gig Hall, most probably that of Whitelee, turned by the River Dane, which was to become exempt from tithe taxes.

Gig Hall is the name of a property on the Staffordshire side of the River Dane, near to Whitelee Farm, which is on the Cheshire side in Wincle parish. A 'gig mill' was another name for a 'fulling mill', as described earlier, so the name of Gig Hall implies that the mill here was a fulling mill, or walkmill, similar to the Danebridge mill of 1671 producing quality cloth.

A millwright named Abraham Bennett, who lived near Macclesfield, was commissioned to build a paper mill, around 1735, at the site on the River Dane where Whitelee Mill stood. It is thought that the mill there had been producing cloth but was now closing down due to competition from other mills in the area. It appears that Bennett had been to see a new 'engine paper mill' in Shropshire and was attempting to copy it at Whitelee. Bennett's attempts to convince his commissioners of the new technology were thwarted by stories that he was not able to complete the mill. However, Bennett had taken on an apprentice in 1733, a certain James Brindley, who was then aged only 17, but was to become a well - known canal engineer. Brindley decided to take a look at the new mill technology himself, and after a day walking there to view it, and then walking back, approximately fifty miles all told, went on to help modify Bennett's plans and complete the building of the engine mill to the satisfaction of all involved. However, not long after completion of the mill, Abraham Bennett died in 1742.

From details of the plans it seems that they were building a paper mill that was based on the use of a machine called a 'Hollander'. This was being introduced into the British paper making industry at the time, having been developed from about 1680 in Holland, and which incorporated what was basically a bathtub with a rotating drum inside which had ridges or spikes. Rags and water were placed into the Hollander, and then it was rotated with the power from the waterwheel of the mill, pulverising the rags into a pulp to ultimately make the paper. Rags were generally the only source of raw material thought capable of being used to make paper prior to the middle of the 19th century.

Whitelee Mill operated with the Hollander system throughout the rest of the 18th century, but by 1834 the mill was becoming obsolete, mainly due to newer technologies, but also after some problems with the rights to use the river to power the waterwheel. The owners of the mill had entered into an agreement with the Trent and Mersey Canal Company to transfer the water rights, with the understanding that the mill would be demolished after the implementation of the agreement. The mill was not demolished then but it was simply closed down and left abandoned to become derelict. There is no evidence of the mill building itself today, but a weir can be seen across the Dane, with a channel where the headrace and wheelpit would have been. The central part of the weir was washed away in 1998 floods, having been there for approximately 260 years. It has been rebuilt by the British Waterways at an estimated cost of half a million pounds.

Folly Mill was situated just north of Danebridge, on Clough Brook, a tributary stream of the River Dane from the Cheshire side, in Wincle parish. It was thought to be so called because two other mills built there had been washed away in floods, and it was thought as 'folly' to build a third. The third mill was built at some time between 1780 and 1790 by Abraham Day and was situated about halfway up a wooded gorge on Clough Brook, at a place called Gideon (or Gibbon's) Cliff.

It is thought that this mill also used the Hollander system to make paper from old rags. The manufacture of paper at this time was subject to a complicated taxing structure, so much so that it involved the attention of Excise Tax collectors. It was recorded that excise taxmen were living permanently at Folly Mill. Excise records from 1816 show that there was a Thomas Hope named as the 'master' paper maker, of both Folly Mill and Whitelee Mill, in Wincle parish. It is not clear however, whether he was the owner of the mills or merely a tenant of Abraham Day.

In 1835, Abraham Day died at the age of 95, and this left Thomas Hope, and subsequent members of his family, to continue the operation of Folly Mill. It was in 1860 that ownership of the mill changed hands to John and Matthias Slack. However, by this time, the paper making industry had become a fully mechanised process with new technologies. Machines that had been invented by the 'Fourdinier' brothers, in Staffordshire, had meant that the hand-made processes being used at Folly Mill brought the mill to its closure, mainly due to it not being competitive.

Folly Mill continued operating until 1867, but in 1869 it was left as 'unoccupied'. It was noted in 1923 by James Thornley, a local historian, who claimed he had visited the mill in his youth when it was producing coarse brown paper and blue glazed paper. These were used by grocers and ironmongers to wrap their wares.

Hollander Beater System

A rough sketch of a Hollander

The 'Hollander' was a machine that was developed by the Dutch (hence the name of Hollander) in 1680, which was designed to produce paper pulp from any cellulose material containing plant fibres. It replaced what were known as 'stamp mills' because the Hollander could produce eight days of the stamp mill pulp quantity in one day. However, the stamp mills process produced slightly stronger paper strength than the new Hollander system. The stamp mills used wooden paddles to create pulped fibres and were usually longer and more capable of being saturated than the resulting pulp fibres produced by the Hollander.

The Hollander used metal blades with a chopping action to cut the raw material, which resulted in shorter fibres and weaker paper strength. Often the metal blades beating against each other would produce metal fragments embedded into the paper. In short, although the machinery produced paper material a lot faster, the quality was not as good. The Hollander design was eventually superseded by a machine called a 'Jordan' which was invented in 1858. This new machine used a technique of grounding down raw materials rather than chopping.

The Hollander beater design, as the rough diagram above shows an example, consisted of a circular water raceway with a beating wheel. The beater wheel was made with multiple blades (ridges or spikes in some cases), mounted on an axle shaft. Using a power source such as a mill wheel system to drive the axle, the blades rotated to beat fibrous materials, or rags in most cases, to produce a pulp slurry for paper manufacture.

4.5 *JAMES BRINDLEY (1716 – 1772)   -   Millwright , wheelwright, and canal engineer

James Brindley was born in 1716 in the village of Tunstead, which is situated a few miles from Buxton in Derbyshire, though much of his life was spent in Staffordshire. Although he was born into a fairly well to do family of yeoman farmers and craftsmen, he received little in the way of any formal education and was mainly taught at home by his mother. At the age of 17, he was encouraged by his mother to take up an apprenticeship with the millwright Abraham Bennett in Sutton, near Macclesfield. His family background of craftsmen must have given him an already inherent mechanical mind, as he was soon showing exceptional understanding, skill and ability in solving problems encountered in the workings of the mills of the time. His solving of the new technology problems of the 'Hollander' system incorporated in Whitelee Mill in 1735 went a long way to establishing himself as a reliable and trusted engineer.

At the age of 26, James Brindley set up his own business as a wheelwright in Leek, in 1742. Eight years later, in 1750, he was expanding his business and rented a millwright's premises in Burslem, Stoke-on-Trent, that belonged to the famous pottery family of Wedgwood's. He became lifelong friends with the Wedgwood family from that time on. Two years later, in 1752, he was making his name as a designer of a steam engine for pumping water out of coal pits, at the Wet Earth Colliery in Clifton in Lancashire. In 1755 he had built a machine for a silk mill in Congleton, but it was from the year of 1759 that he was to begin an illustrious career in the work of a canal engineer.

He was called upon by the Duke of Bridgwater to help with the construction of a ten mile stretch of canal, which was to be used to transport coal from the Duke's coal mines in Worsley, to the textile manufacturing centre of Manchester. The Duke already had an engineer working on the project in the form of a John Gilbert, who had heard of Brindley's previous exploits in the coal pits at Clifton and had asked for Brindley to help solve some problems that were being encountered in the construction of the canal. Brindley came up with a plan for an underground channel that ran from the coal mines to the head of the canal at Worsley, and then planned an aqueduct at Barton which took the canal over the River Irwell to enable the link into Manchester. The 'Bridgewater' canal, as it was called, was regarded by many as the first British canal of the 'modern era', but much of the work has since been accredited to John Gilbert, who was also the Duke of Bridgewater's land agent.

However, James Brindley's reputation had been enhanced, and the success of the canal encouraged similar projects to be given to Brindley to work on. He helped to extend the Bridgewater Canal to Runcorn, and in turn it was further extended to join the major work of the Trent and Mersey Canal. Around 1762, James Brindley had moved to a residence in the north of Stoke on Trent, called Turnhurst Hall. This was situated between the areas of Great Chell and Packmoor, a site which is now only noted for a pub called the 'Brindley Lock'. He was to use the grounds of the residence to experiment with the designs for canal locks, which up to this time was something he had not built on canal sites.

Brindley also came up with a plan that he believed would link up the four great rivers of England with canals. He wanted to join the Mersey, the Trent, the Severn, and the Thames rivers with what he had called 'the "Grand Cross" scheme'. After his experiments with lock building at Turnhurst, in 1762 he set out to Chester to make survey sketches to link the River Dee to Whitchurch in Shropshire. His friendship with the Wedgwood family, whose main interests were in the success of the pottery industry, made their support for a connection through Staffordshire to link the Trent and Mersey more amicable, especially as it would mean improved transport for pottery wares, which at the time was mainly dealt with by the use of pack horses.

In 1765, on the 08th of December, James Brindley got married to Anne Henshall. He was 49 years old, but Anne was only 19. Her brother, Hugh Henshall, was involved in the construction of the Worsley to Manchester Canal about five years earlier, and it was through him that James Brindley got to meet Anne. They were married at Wolstanton Church, near Newcastle under Lyme, and had two daughters, Anne and Susannah. However, there is an unconfirmed report that James had previously had a son by a Mary Bennett in 1760. Mary Bennett is listed as the mother, but the father is listed as unknown, to a child called John Bennett. John Bennett (1760 – 1799) had a direct descendant born in 1867 in Stoke on Trent, by the name of (Enoch) Arnold Bennett, who became a famed novelist.

Back at his house at Turnhurst, Brindley had been experimenting with lock building and had come up with an idea for a design for a 'narrow' lock, which was to become characteristic of most of the canals in the Midlands. They were designed in relation to the elongated boats that had been incorporated in his earlier work at the coal mines of Worsley and the underground channel there. The canal boats were originally called 'the starvationers', but subsequently, and more simply, they became known as the 'narrowboats'.

Brindley's work on the 'Grand Cross' scheme continued, and from Runcorn the canal building would need his new lock design to be used, on a section with a series of 35 locks. This went uphill, and then the canal was to continue towards Stoke on Trent, where at nearby Kidsgrove there were plans for a tunnel to be built. This was to be 3000 yards long, and the longest canal tunnel to be planned at that time, known as Harecastle Tunnel. On the other side the canal was to continue and join up with the river Trent, but not until it joined at Wilden Ferry, near Shardlow, north of Castle Donnington.

The Harecastle Tunnel proved to be one project that Brindley did not see finished. He had so many other canal building projects going on at the same time. Working on the Chesterfield canal, started in 1771, he was out surveying a section between Leek and Froghall when he was caught out in a heavy rain storm. This was a regular occurrence whilst he was surveying, but this time he had developed a chill and doctors attending him discovered he had developed diabetes. His health took a downward turn and he never recovered, resulting in his death on 27th September 1772. Only a week earlier the final section of the Birmingham Canal had been completed, but it took another five years, with the help of Thomas Telford, before the Harecastle Tunnel was completed. Coal was finally transported from the Midlands to the Thames at Oxford in January 1790, nearly 18 years after Brindley's death.

He was buried on the 30th September 1772, at St. James Church in the village of Newchapel, not far from Kidsgrove and the Harecastle Tunnel, and near to his home of Turnhurst. There is also a nearby village called Brindley Ford, which I assume is named in dedication to him. Throughout his life, James Brindley had helped to build 365 miles of canals, along with numerous watermills. One of his mills at Leek now houses the 'Brindley Water Museum'. His canals included not only the Manchester canal and the Trent and Mersey canal, but also the Oxford canal, the Coventry canal, the Birmingham canal, and the Staffordshire and Worcestershire canal.

The Staffordshire and Worcestershire Canal is especially important to me, as part of the canal begins a link to my next adventures of discovering Staffordshire, as I head to south Staffordshire and discover the historical stories around Kinver. The village of Kinver lies near to the river Stour, and the Staffordshire and Worcestershire canal links northwards up through Wolverhampton, and Stafford to join the Trent and Mersey canal near to Shugborough Hall. It is only now that I can appreciate how much effort must have been involved, within such a short space of time, as the work of James Brindley achieved so much in only 22 years of canal building.

4.6 *THE BROCKLEHURST BARONETCY of SWYTHAMLEY

The Brocklehurst family are first mentioned in the history of Heaton 'manor' in 1832, when the Swythamley Grange was bought by John Brocklehurst. He was a successful silk weaver and had become Member of Parliament for Macclesfield. He was the younger brother of William Coare Brocklehurst who had also been the MP for Macclesfield.

The 'manor' of Heaton had been held by Dieulacres Abbey since 1535, when the 'manor' was deemed to be a tract of land which is granted with rights of inheritance by a Royal Charter. The manor had been sold in two 'grange' parts to various parties over the years, with both Fairborough and Swythamley having been granges belonging to the abbey. When the Brocklehurst family still held the Swythamley grange on 27th August 1903, it was decreed that the Brocklehurst's were to be given a family title of a 'baronetcy'. This was initially created for the great nephew of John Brocklehurst, namely Philip Lancaster Brocklehurst who was 76 years old. He was named as the 1st Baronet of Swythamley Park, but this was only to last for one year as he died in 1904.

He was succeeded by his eldest son, Philip Lee Brocklehurst. At only seventeen years old, he was born in 1887 when his father was sixty years of age. He was soon to go to Cambridge University, where he would study geology and meet Ernest Shackleton, who was involved with the Royal Geographical Society in an attempt to put together an expedition of his own to the Antarctic, having already been there with Captain Scott in 1902. Philip Lee Brocklehurst took part in Shackleton's expedition in 1907-1909 as an assistant geologist, though some reports suggest he funded £2,000 towards the expedition so as to secure his place.

Philip Lee Brocklehurst married on his return from the Antarctic in 1913, but his marriage to Gladys Murray was later dissolved, even though he had two daughters. Alas he had no son, and heir, so the title of baronet was passed down to his sister's son, John Ogilvy Brocklehurst. His father, Henry, had been killed in action in Burma in the Second World War.

Philip Lee Brocklehurst died in 1975, and John Ogilvy Brocklehurst died in 1981 with no heir to continue the Baronetcy, and so the title then became extinct.

Sir Philip Lee Brocklehurst and the Shackleton Expedition

Ernest Shackleton led an expedition to reach the South Pole, having tried to secure £30,000 funding from the Royal Geographical Society and other private sources of friends and acquaintances. It was a struggle to get backing, but eventually he had enough, if not all, support to embark on the journey. This included the £2,000 from Brocklehurst, though he was officially taken on the expedition as an assistant geologist, and not as a paying guest as it had been suggested by some. The initial journey was supposed to begin in the summer of 1907, using a ship by the name of 'The Nimrod'. The ship left for New Zealand on 11th August 1907, but Shackleton was still sorting supplies and finance so had to catch up with the Nimrod in New Zealand. On the 1st January 1908, 'The Nimrod', was towed nearly 1400 miles by a steamship, provided by secured backing from the New Zealand government, before it was released to make its own way to Ross Island at the edge of Antarctica.

The ship was overloaded with ten ponies – none of which survived the expedition, nine dogs, an Arrol–Johnston motor car – which was the first car to be driven in the Antarctic, a supply hut, and food that was enough to last supposedly for two years. Seven weeks after leaving New Zealand, the Nimrod reached Ross Island where the expedition hut was set up at Cape Royds. The Nimrod returned to New Zealand for safe harbour so as not to be crushed by the ice packs of the cold Antarctic sea.

At the beginning of March 1908, Brocklehurst and five others, though not including Shackleton, set out to climb Mount Erebus, an active volcano. Diary records were kept telling that on 08th March they had reached 8750 feet, when the temperature was 20 degrees below zero, but a blizzard of snow was hampering efforts causing the team to stay in their sleeping bags all day. They had left behind all the tent poles because of the weight so none of the tents could be erected upright and were used mainly as cover over their sleeping bags. There was no ready supply of water, or warm food, because they were unable to light the camp stoves, and it was a difficult day made worse for Brocklehurst when he attempted to venture out of his sleeping bag to check on the weather.

For some reason, Brocklehurst had chosen to wear normal ski boots and not the warmer reindeer skin boots being worn by his companions. Consequently, he soon became a victim of frost bite, but the next day, which was his 21st birthday and he celebrated with a biscuit and a piece of chocolate, the weather had improved enough for the rest of the team to continue the task of climbing an almost vertical gradient up to the summit of the volcano. Brocklehurst had no alternative but to stay behind due to his frost-bitten feet. Steps had to be cut into the ice with ice axes and the summit of Mount Erebus and crater edge was not reached until the next day, the 10th March 1908. They had become the first men to climb the mountain of Antarctica.

They came down from the summit to meet up with Brocklehurst, who despite his frostbite was determined to carry his own gear back down to the expedition hut at Cape Royds. The weather turned again, into another blizzard, and they were seen struggling along by Shackleton who ran out to meet them shouting – "Did you get to the top?". They were cheered back into camp after their news and celebrated with champagne and a hot 'welcome home' meal.

Unfortunately for Brocklehurst, frost bite had taken hold in one of his big toes and had to be amputated by Dr. Marshall on the 06th April. He was then put into Shackleton's quarters for recuperation.

It wasn't until 05th October 1908 that a three-man team was sent out to reach the Magnetic Pole, and it was not until the 29th October that Shackleton led the South Pole expedition. Obviously, the weather was playing an important part in decisions as this was now summer in the southern hemisphere. Shackleton's party also had a support team following behind, which included Brocklehurst. A diary of events was being kept by Frank Wild, but he became snow-blind for a time and it was Brocklehurst who continued his diary. When Wild had recovered, he read what Brocklehurst had been writing, and at least one page was torn from the diary because of what he described later as 'lurid details' of the journey.

On the 7th November 1908, the support team were told to go back to Cape Royds, leaving Shackleton and his small team to continue on to the South Pole. However, with food supplies running low, and the weather getting colder, it wasn't long before they realised they were not going to reach the South Pole.

On the 9th January 1909, they recorded their position as - 88 deg. 23 min. South, longitude of 162 degrees – but still 97 miles short of the South Pole. They turned back, marking the spot with a Union Jack flag, and a brass cylinder that contained some stamps and documents. Meanwhile, the Magnetic Pole team had reached their goal on the 15th January 1909, which in some ways made up for the disappointment for Shackleton's failure to reach the South Pole. At least, he also had the consolation of knowing that he had recorded the furthest travelled distance south record, previously set by Captain Scott in 1902, as he had been a member of that expedition too.

4.7 * Brocklehurst's Wallabies - the Roaches and the Winking Man

The Baronetcy of the Brocklehurst family had begun in 1903 with Philip Lancaster Brocklehurst (1827 – 1904), who had been the supplier of the land and materials for the construction of the present bridge at Danebridge in 1869. He had in turn been the son of John Brocklehurst, who had been a Liberal Member of Parliament for Macclesfield for 36 years between 1832 and 1868, before he died two years later in 1870, aged 81.

Not more than 400 metres from the bridge at Danebridge, into Cheshire, is the village of Wincle, where a pub is now called 'The Ship Inn'. It has a sign hanging outside that depicts the 'Nimrod' in the Antarctic ice as a tribute to the exploits of Philip Lee Brocklehurst and the Ernest Shackleton expedition. On their return from the Antarctic in 1909, Shackleton was best man for Sir Philip Lee Brocklehurst's marriage to Gladys Murray in 1913. Unfortunately, this marriage was later dissolved, and having no son it was his nephew John Ogilvy Brocklehurst who succeeded the title of Baronet in 1975.

From the expedition, which was part funded by the New Zealand government, the personal sledging flag of Philip Lee Brocklehurst is now displayed in the Antarctic Gallery of Lyttleton Museum in New Zealand. It features his family arms, along with three 'brocks', or badgers. For his part in the expedition, Brocklehurst was honoured with a medal from the Royal Geographical Society.

When he died in 1975, aged 88, he was succeeded as Baronet by John Ogilvy Brocklehurst. His father was Henry Courtney Brocklehurst, who was a Lieutenant–Colonel, and an airplane pilot in the Second World War, but was unfortunately killed in action by the Japanese in Burma in 1942, aged 54. Henry had previously been a game warden to the Government of Sudan and had started a private zoo back in England near the family home of Swythamley, at Roaches Hall, near Upper Hulme.

In 1940, wartime regulations were given to close down all private zoos. It was suggested that the Brocklehurst zoo was to be closed, and in the process a number of animals either escaped or were set free. Among the animals that escaped were three yaks, a Nilgai antelope, and five 'Bennetts' wallabies. The wallabies found their way onto the moorlands around the Roaches, and the Winking Man rock formation. It was a few years later when it was noticed that the number of wallabies had increased, and by 1963 it was thought there were about 50 animals. However, in the winter of 1963, there were very deep snow falls and it was very cold, and the number of wallabies declined virtually overnight.

There were some sightings of the wallabies over the years, and traditionally their stronghold was the wilderness of the Roaches between Leek and Buxton. There have been sightings in the River Dove valley, as they prefer areas where there is wild water, but numbers were down to about 14 in 1985, and only six sightings in 1992, then only three in 1995. They were thought to have all died but there have been sightings as far away as Burton on Trent, and at an area called Kinder Scout – a moorland plateau in north Derbyshire, where a pair of wallabies were spotted together. The last sighting with photographic evidence of a wallaby was made on 02nd August 2009, by a David Hobson from Buxton, who was walking at 7 a.m. near the Hangingstone Rock, not far from Swythamley Hall. The last sighting was made near Lud's Church, in April of this year, 2015.

So, this is my link to my next walk. A walk maybe in search of a Brocklehurst wallaby, maybe one is near to the Roaches, the Winking Man, or the Dove valley. The prospects are slim at best, but one never knows what one will find in Staffordshire.

DISCOVERING STAFFORDSHIRE

An Historical Companion Guide

To Walking In North Staffordshire

Winking Man, Dove Head, and Hollinsclough Village

(Walk No. GM05 – July)

The main approach for this long walk was to highlight the scenic qualities of the Staffordshire Moorlands, starting with the iconic 'Winking Man' rock formation on the 'Roaches'. Then after a somewhat dangerous trek along the main road, having to avoid large lorries, up to Flash Bar, taking in the views of an almost barren-like moorlands, I had a more relaxed and pleasant scenic stroll down the upper Dove river valley to reach Hollinsclough village, with its views of the hills in Derbyshire. Continuing the walk up and down valleys, into the Manifold river valley to the hamlet of Hardings Booth and from there the smaller valley of Oakenclough Brook took me to Newtown village, before making the long trek back to the 'Winking Man'.

My internet research threw up an interesting fact about this walk, in that by starting at the Winking Man pub (9th), almost immediately followed by a pub called the Royal Cottage (6th), then walking up to Flash where we have already seen the New Inn pub (5th), and the Knights Table (3rd) at Flash bar, we have four of the top ten highest pubs in the UK within four kilometres on, or near to, the A53, between Leek and Flash, in Staffordshire.

Highest pubs in the UK – 1. Tan Hill Inn, (1730ft), Swaledale, N.Yorks. 2. The Cat and Fiddle, (1690ft), A537 between Buxton and Macclesfield. 3. Travellers Rest (Knights Table), (1500ft), A53 near Flash. 4. Kirkstone Pass Inn, (1480ft), A592 between Windermere and Patterdale. 5. The New Inn, (1470ft), in Flash village. 6. Royal Cottage, (1460ft), A53 between Leek and Buxton. 7. Wanlockhead Inn, (1440ft), in Wanlockhead village, B797 in Dumfrieshire. 8. The Mermaid Inn, (1440ft), Morridge road, between Newtown and Thornicliffe, near Leek. 9. The Winking Man Inn, (1440ft), A53 between Leek and Buxton. 10.Sportsmans Arms, (1430ft), A543 between Bylchau and Pentrefoelas, near Denbigh, N. Wales.

Walking along the A53 was a little daunting, as there is no real footpath to speak of, and a constant flow of heavy lorry traffic from Buxton causes a little anxiety when the airflow almost drags you into their path as they pass by. In hindsight, it would have been safer to take the smaller side road after Morridge Top Farm past the Brand Plantation to get to Flash Bar, and maybe a little more scenic.

Locating Dove Head Farm on the Derbyshire border was the beginning of the more pleasant part of this walk. Though not necessarily the actual source of the River Dove, a small stream here forms the beginning of the Dove valley. A somewhat difficult trek along disappearing footpaths with obscure signposts made the valley walk a little disconcerting, but perseverance is the key and with some small changes to the intended route I eventually arrived at Hollinsclough village. A small village, but a pleasant enough place, with great views of Chrome Hill in Derbyshire beyond the Methodist church and school.

The distance factor of this walk starts to kick in with a steep uphill climb out of the Dove valley, via Coatestown, into the Manifold valley. Then another climb, up the small valley of Oakenclough Brook, takes me to the village of Newtown, which is under the jurisdiction of the township and parish of Fawfieldhead. Here there is a small converted Methodist church, and the larger St. Paul's church which have some aesthetic appeal.

I would like to thank the residents of Highfield House, for replenishing my water bottle and giving me a large cold glass of water on what was turning into an unexpectedly very warm day, before I made another trek down the small valley to pass Oakenclough Hall Farm and reach the road back to the 'Winking Man'.

(Note: - I had intended to walk along this road back to the Royal Cottage pub, but a passing van driver stopped for directions to the Winking Man pub and gave me a lift back to my start point, and so my walk terminated here officially).

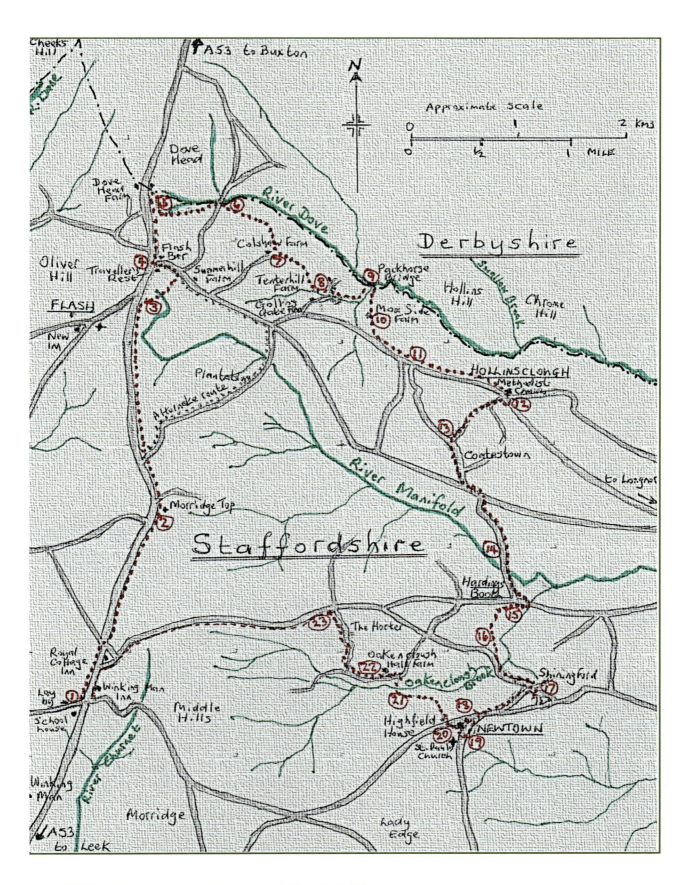

Walk GM05 – Winking Man, Dove Head and Hollinsclough Village

102

Drive to the start point using the A53 Leek to Buxton Road, travelling from Leek you will soon come to the iconic sight of the 'Winking Man' rock formation on your left, which is soon followed by the pub on the right, also called the Winking Man. However, having found that the car park is prone to clamping unless previous permission to park is obtained, I turned left just before the pub to find a small lay-by about 50 metres on the right, and parked up accordingly. (Grid Ref. SK 02455 63635).

Walk Details

Start with a superb view of the 'Winking Man' rocks, and a slightly hazardous walk on the side of the busy A53 road up to Flash Bar. Then trek down the upper valley of the River Dove starting from Dove Head Farm to the village of Hollinsclough. Across country then, up and down valleys to the River Manifold at the hamlet of Hardings Booth, and to the village of Newtown. Down into the valley of Oakenclough Brook and up to the road that leads back to the Winking Man.

The walk is about 14kms, or 8 ¾ miles, and would take about 7 hours to complete. Some muddy patches and some steep incline sections, but generally not too difficult. Busy road section to start with needs care.

1) - Having parked in the lay-by opposite the Winking Man pub, walk back to the main road, the A53, and turn left towards Buxton, but I advise crossing the road to the side of oncoming traffic due to the heavy lorry traffic. Walk carefully, keeping an eye on oncoming traffic at all times as there is a lack of a proper footpath, and the grass verge is quite overgrown. As previously mentioned, the Winking Man pub is the ninth highest pub in the UK, and very soon after starting the walk you come to the Royal Cottage pub, which is the sixth highest pub in the UK, yet I didn't notice any change in height on the road.

Royal Cottage Pub

2) – Continue walking on the verge of the A53 for approximately ¾ mile until you come to a small group of buildings at the next road junction on the left. To the right of this you will see what looks like a barn building, which is marked on the map as a church. I believe this was, at some point in history, a Methodist chapel. It is now part of Morridge Top Farm.

Morridge Top Farm building, site of the old Methodist chapel

3) – Continue walking on the A53 for another mile, until you reach the junction for Flash village to the left. Just past this, on the right, you should see a public footpath sign pointing right across the field. Also, there is a small wooden gate to allow you entry into the field, however there are cows here and I decided to climb over the fence into the field on the left to avoid any confrontation. Following the fence, with another climb over into the next field, all of which are a bit muddy, you come to a small road and a farm called Summerhill. In hindsight, as previously mentioned, it would have been better to take a right turn after Morridge Top farm to Brand Plantation and reach Summerhill along a quiet road avoiding heavy traffic and a couple of fence climbs.

*- (Walk time here about one hour)

Summerhill Farm

4) – Turn left on the road after viewing Summerhill Farm, walk for about 200 metres where you will see The Knight's Table pub (also known as the Traveller's Rest) as seen in the previous walk around Flash. Re-joining the main A53 road, walk about 400 metres along to the border of Derbyshire, where the last building is Dove Head Farm. There are houses at the bottom of the hill, when walking back into Staffordshire, which include Quarnford Lodge. Opposite here on your left, an open gateway with a footpath signpost points downhill into the Dove valley.

5) – Head into the grassy area, though the footpath is not clear here, keeping right as much as possible. You will soon see a small area with wild flowers where a stream seems to trickle out from. (I am convinced this is a source of the River Dove).

Possible source of the River Dove, near Dove Head Farm

    A faint footpath can be seen with a wire fence to the right; walk along the path until it comes in line with a track/drive where you can also see a stile. However, when going over the stile, the path seems to disappear again, so walk across the field heading slightly left towards some telephone poles. It becomes very boggy at the bottom of the slope where the River Dove begins trickling on your left. Over another stile here puts you on to a road, where you turn left and head towards a small stone bridge about 50 metres away. The River Dove trickles under the bridge, and to the right there is a footpath sign with a stile to negotiate. Climb over the stile and follow the faint path, with the river on your left and a stone wall on your right. The path rises uphill to another stile, but you should keep straight on here following the line of the telephone wires up to yet another stile.

6) – Climb over this stile into a field, then keeping to the side of the field, where you should see a farmhouse, the path veers right away from the river. Go through a farm gate onto a track. There are sheep in the field to your left but follow the path until another stile is seen on your right. This has a yellow marker on it denoting a public footpath. However, there are horses in the field when you climb this stile so keep to the left, but then follow the wall/fence boundary as it goes to the right and uphill to another stile.

7) – Climb over this stile into another field, where looking ahead, slightly uphill you should spot another stile. From this stile you should be able to see a gap in a stone wall. Head for this gap, but you should also see a gate and a footpath post with another yellow arrow pointing across the next field. The footpath goes downhill, then between two crumbling stone walls, heading down towards another farmhouse which has a barn in need of repair to the right. It also gets very wet and muddy on the way down, as you should soon see a gate, but also gaps in the wall on your left.

*(Walk time here, approximately 2 and ¼ hours).

8) – Go through the gate, or a gap in the wall, turning left keeping a wire fence on your right. A stream can be heard trickling below, and it is very boggy and wet underfoot here. You will have to duck under low tree branches too as you walk along the stream side, around a large tree where cow footprints are a plenty, until you come to a drive/track on your right. You should see the drive leading to a small road at a gate, so head for the gate which you will have to climb over.

9) - To your right there are farm buildings, part of Golling Gate Farm. To the left there is Tenterhill Farm, which is the direction you need to go. Just at the farmyard entrance look to the right where you should see a path leading down the side of the farm, with a stream on the right of it. Follow this path, which goes between stone walls heading downhill. It starts off being wet and muddy, but soon becomes dry and rocky. At the bottom of the track it levels out and becomes wet and muddy again and the stream flows under your feet into the River Dove. It also brings you to a delightful little stone bridge.

Old packhorse bridge over the River Dove, near Tenterhill Farm

10) - Just before the stream joins the River Dove, you will see a stile to your right, where a path leads steeply uphill with a fence into a field. Walk up the steep field to find a gap in a stone wall leading into another field. Beware of cows in this field but following what seems like a dirt pathway across the field and heading for the corner of the field where there is a gate and some stone steps in a wall. Go through the gate on to a driveway, which belongs to Moorside Farm. At the end of the drive you come to a small tarmac road, where you turn left. Walk along this road taking in the views of Derbyshire to your left, which are some of the best views on this walk, as the road descends down to Hollinsclough village.

View of Derbyshire hills, Hollins Hill and Chrome Hill, from the road into Hollinsclough.

11) - The road goes downhill for approximately half a mile, or one kilometre, with the views of Hollins Hill and the smaller pointed Chrome Hill to your left on the Derbyshire side of the River Dove valley. Just on the left as you enter the village you should see the Hollinsclough Methodist chapel. There is a plaque dated 1801 and with the name of Bethel J.L. above the doorway. Subsequent research finds that the chapel was listed on 1st February 1967 as a Grade II building, but as a Bethel Chapel, which is investigated further in my research pages. The J.L. refers to the builder of the chapel, and minister, John Lomas (1747-1823).

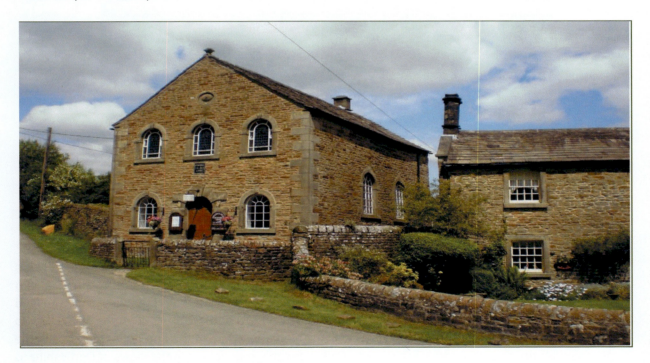

Hollinsclough Methodist (Bethel) Chapel, 1801

12) - Just a little further on the left, turning left at the junction is the Hollinsclough primary school, which also has some interesting features. It also had a unique system introduced into its teaching methods, since it was nearly closed down with only 5 pupils registered at one time. It now has about 50 pupils who travel from as far as Stockport and Holmes Chapel to attend, but the pupils also do some home learning called 'flexi-schooling' apparently. It warranted some research on the internet to clarify this. (See topics sections).

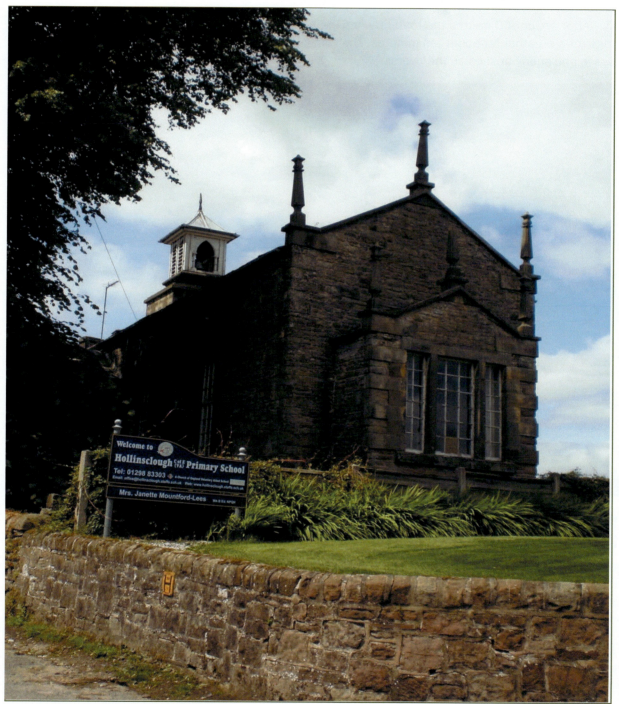

Hollinsclough Primary School

*- (Walk time here – approximately 3 ½ hours)

13) - Walk back to the road junction, where you will see just opposite the church a sign for 'Home Farm', with a track/road going uphill. Walk past some cottages then the track divides left and right. Keep right here, going steeply uphill for about half a mile. The track is sandy and slightly rocky under foot but not too difficult. At the top of the hill the track meets a road, which is at a bend. Take a right turn here along the road until you reach a road junction about 200 metres along. Turn left at the junction, where you will pass Coatestown Cottage. Keep walking straight on, the road then comes to another junction where you turn left, then about 50 metres or so take the next right junction heading downhill into the Manifold valley.

14) – After about 500 metres the road reaches the River Manifold, where I sat awkwardly on a wooden bridge for a breather for about ten minutes. The valley upriver is fairly pleasing to the eye with its marsh grasses and shady bushes on the riverside.

View of River Manifold valley near Hardings Booth

15) - The road crosses the river and continues down to a junction about 100 metres along, where the hamlet of Hardings Booth is situated. There are a few old farm buildings here to see, and another tributary stream that joins the River Manifold a little further down from Bridge House Farm. From the junction, turning slightly right and uphill, cross the road where you should see a small wooden gate and a footpath post with the words 'Concession Path to avoid Farm Buildings'.

16) - Go through the gate and walk uphill using the steps to another gate into a field. Keep slightly left here looking for a public footpath post in the field near some small trees, then continue across the field with the farm buildings to your left until you come to a gate. Veer right through the gate, into a muddy area which leads to the field on the right, but I had to duck under some tape to follow the public footpath post which appears straight ahead of you. With the tributary stream to the left and a stone wall on the right, head along the grassy area aiming for the stream, where a gate with a footpath marker comes into view. Go through the gate, then walk on keeping the wall to your left heading for the corner of the field where a stile comes into view just before a small road.

Bridge House Farm, in Hardings Booth hamlet.

17) - At the road, turn left and walk towards the house on the left of the stream. This is another tributary stream to the river Manifold called Oakenclough Brook and the house is known as 'Shining Ford'.

Shining Ford House on the bank of Oakenclough Brook

18) - From 'Shining Ford' house, keep walking along the road uphill to a crossroads, where there is an old schoolhouse. Turn right here, walking for about 200 metres behind a farmhouse when the road comes to another junction. Keeping right you should see Holly Grove Farm, which is used by a coal dealer, then just a little further on the left you will see an old red telephone box outside a house on the corner of the road junction. The buildings here form part of the village of Newtown, and part of the parish and township of 'Fawfieldhead'. The house is a converted Methodist chapel, and by walking around the back, turning left at the road junction, which is the road to Warslow, you can get a clear view of its past purpose.

Converted Methodist chapel at Newtown

*- (Walk time to here – about 5 hours)

19) – Continue on the Warslow road for another 200 metres, where the road forks at a bend. On the right you see the other Newtown church. This is St. Paul's church, Newtown, in the township of Fawfieldhead, and is still used as a church today.

St. Paul's Church, Newtown (Fawfieldhead)

20) – Having taken the right fork here before the church, there is a pathway to the side of a house at the top of the incline, with a field to the right. A footpath arrow should be easy to see by a stone wall, then following the pathway to the left it leads to a field where you can see a house beyond the field at about 250 metres. Head for this house, which is Belfield House, when, at the edge of the field you should see a gap in the wall to get you onto the road. Turn right onto the road, slightly downhill for about 100 metres to Highfield House on your left. This has a date stone on it of 1993-94, built by E.Mellor, and the occupants were kind enough to fill my water bottle for me now that the sun was shining down strongly.

Highfield House, built by E.Mellor

21) – Just past this house, on the left, is a footpath which leads to a field. Then there is a track which bends slightly left, and veers right downhill towards the brook, Oakenclough Brook. Some farm buildings can be seen on the opposite bank of the brook. A small bridge here goes over the brook and has a date stone on it, marked 'E.S. 1871'. After the bridge there is a gate, and pathway, and a further gate. Watch out for the cows here, especially those with a calf, which I think was a Belgian Blue cow.

'Belgian Blue' cow, and her calf, near Oakenclough Brook.

112

Oakenclough Brook

22) - Turn left just before the main farm building, which is Oakenclough Hall Farm, onto a track that has a wire fence on the left. Keep following this track until you reach a cattle grid, where it meets another track just past it. Turn right here onto the track, over another cattle grid, and then keep going along here, past two farm houses, until the track meets up with the road.

  *(Walk Time, approximately 5 ½ hours)

23) - At this point, turning left along the road will lead all the way back to the Royal Cottage Inn, and the Winking Man, approximately 1 ½ miles, however I was stopped by a van driver asking for directions to the Winking Man so I kindly accepted a lift back along this road to my start point, thus ending my walk.

  *(Estimated total walk time, approximately 6 hours to 6 ½ hours).

The iconic 'Winking Man' rock formation

5.1 Walking Through The Ancient Parish Townships Of Alstonefield

5.2 Heathylee Township   - A Brief History

                                              - Mary, The Maid of the Inn

5.3 Rock Hall Cottage and Doxey Pool

5.4 The Roaches

5.5 Hollinsclough Township   - A Brief History

5.6 John Lomas

5.7 Bethel and Jacob's Ladder

5.8 Education in Hollinsclough   - Flexi Schooling

5.9 Fawfieldhead Township   - A Brief History

View of Hollinsclough village

5.1 *Walking Through The Ancient Parish Townships Of Alstonefield

The route of this fifth walk takes me into four of the seven townships that formed the ancient parish of Alstonefield. Beginning in the township of 'Heathylee', near to the 'Winking Man' rock formation that is part of Ramshaw Rocks, the walk then heads north into the familiar territory of 'Quarnford' township. Continuing up to the Derbyshire border and the head of the River Dove, the walk then follows the River Dove valley, then goes into the township, and village, of 'Hollinsclough', before crossing back into the northern part of Heathylee. Latterly, the walk then brings me to the fourth township, that of Fawfieldhead, where after a visit to the village of Newtown and the valley of Oakenclough Brook the route comes back into Heathylee township and back to the Winking Man.

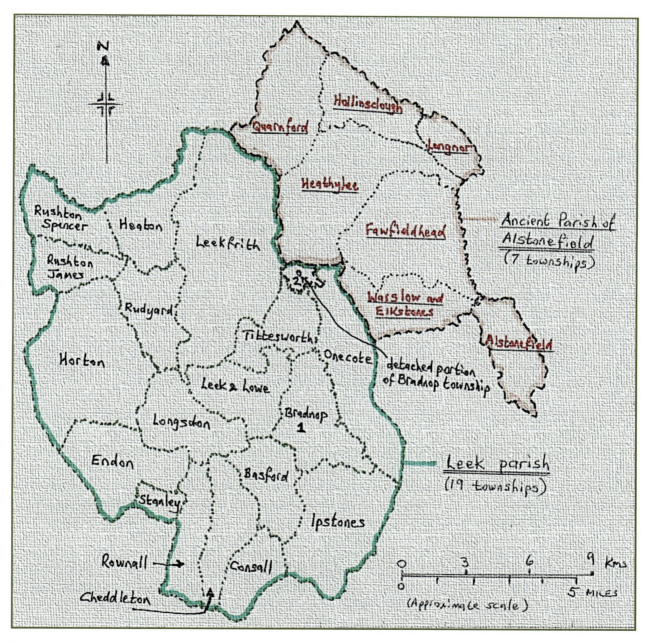

Diagram showing the seven townships of the Ancient Parish of Alstonefield , as well as the approximate locations of the nineteen townships of Leek parish, that includes a detached portion of Bradnop township that lies to the south of Heathylee.

116

The 'ancient parish' of Alstonefield lay in the north-east corner of the county of Staffordshire. An 'ancient parish' is defined as one that existed firstly for ecclesiastical purposes, as an area under the jurisdiction of a clergyman with 'cure of souls', but which gained secular functions in later periods. The first secular function was the relief of the poor, which under successive statutory authorities began with the poor law of 1597. Therefore, the term 'ancient parish' is used for a parish which existed before 1597 and which thereafter served both secular and ecclesiastical roles. Also, after 1597, 'ecclesiastical parishes' came into existence which were used to serve only the ecclesiastical role, as opposed to the 'civil parishes' which were set up to cater for only the secular, or civil roles, which were commonly defined as areas where 'a separate poor rate is, or could be, assessed'.

Alstonefield was the second largest ancient parish in the county, after Leek. There was a church in the village of Alstonefield before the Norman Conquest, but it was Longnor that became the main settlement in the manor of Alstonefield parish, with a chapel there by the 12th century, and a market and a fair by 1293. The townships of Heathylee, Quarnford, Hollinsclough and Fawfieldhead (the four townships covered in my walk) lay in what was called in 1227 as, the 'Forest of Alstonefield'. A forest existed in the area in the 12th century, and later it was known as the 'forest of Mauban'. This was called 'Malbank Frith' in the early 14th century, after the Malbank family who were lords of Alstonefield manor up until 1176. A name of 'Malbon Frith' was also used for an area of wasteland until the late 16th century.

In the mid 1270's, there were three Lords of Alstonefield who jointly claimed 'view of frankpledge', which basically entailed gathering the population into groups of ten households (a tithing) for the purposes of taxes and self-policing. A single 'manor court' was still used for the whole manor, but jurisdiction was exercised by the lords with two main shares from the three. The court held in 1530, was in the name of the Blounts, who were lords of one of the two main shares, and from 1545 the court was held in the name of Vincent Mundy, who held both main shares. In 1697, the Alstonefield court was held at 'Hayesgate' in Fawfieldhead township and was still held there at its last recorded sitting in 1853.

For taxing and poor rating purposes, the ancient parish had been divided into three parts by 1403. One part consisted of Alstonefield township, a second part was called High Frith, which covered Fawfieldhead, Heathylee, Quarnford, and Hollinsclough townships, and the third part consisted of Longnor, Warslow, and Lower and Upper Elkstone. The four townships of High Frith became separate townships in 1733, having decided to relieve the poor with separate arrangements. Longnor was a separate township by the late 17th century, leaving 'Warslow and Elkstones' township to its own devices.

In the 1630's, the whole ancient parish was characterized by smallholdings which were being set up for agricultural purposes. There was, and still is today, a large area of moorland waste land, which was considered as suitable only for rough grazing. Alstonefield township itself was lucky enough to have three times as much farmland as it had waste land, with Longnor township having two thirds of its land area dedicated to farm pasture. Cottagers were allowed to settle on wasteland in the High Frith townships, so as to improve the land, but only at their own expense. The cottagers were rewarded by having smaller rents to pay as tenants of the land they had settled.

By the end of the 16th century, the parish of Alstonefield was under the lordship of the Harpur family, who came from Swarkestone, south of Derby. For more than 350 years most of the manor stayed in the ownership of the family, though the name was changed from Harpur to Crewe, and then to 'Harpur-Crewe'. The manor was still being held by them until 1981 when the grandson of the last baronet was forced to sell the estate due to in heritance tax. It was thought by some that they held very little regard for the tenants of the land, as they rarely visited the parish of Alstonefield, and many quotes seem to uphold this contempt, including Sir George Crewe' comments in 1819/20 about his tenants –

"they are, 100 years behind the rest of the world, well-disposed but ignorant and simple minded".

5.2 *Heathylee Township - A Brief History

The western boundary of the township of 'Heathylee' is formed by two streams, Back Brook and Black Brook. The smaller Back Brook flows south into the River Churnet, whilst two forks of Black Brook, as seen before in my first walk, flow west into the River Dane near Gradbach. Beyond the western boundary is Leek parish and the township of Leekfrith, along with its other eighteen townships.

The River Churnet begins its course from the water table in an area of Staffordshire Moorland just behind the Royal Cottage Inn, flowing down the east side of the main Leek to Buxton road, the A53, past the Ramshaw rocks, until it crosses under the road into the village of Upper Hulme and out of the township into the Tittesworth Reservoir and beyond. The Royal Cottage Inn, built around 1805, was thought to have been renamed in 1833. It was thought to have been a house where Prince Charles Edward Stuart slept during a visit in 1745. The prince had stayed in Leek, but there is no confirmation of him staying at the Cottage Inn, yet it was later renamed with the adopted royal name.

To the north of the township is the valley of the River Manifold, which begins its course in Quarnford township near to Flash village and twelve miles later it joins the River Dove just beyond the village of Ilam. In the southern part of the township is the smaller valley of Oakenclough Brook, which flows into the Manifold near the hamlet of Hardings Booth. In between the valley of Oakenclough Brook and the River Churnet, the land rises steeply to a height of over 1500 feet forming a ridge of land known as Morridge. The highest point is found near to Morridge Top Farm, where there used to be a Primitive Methodist chapel, but is now just a barn. The lowest point in the township is near to another Methodist chapel, to the south in the village of Upper Hulme, which sits near the River Churnet at 825 feet above sea level.

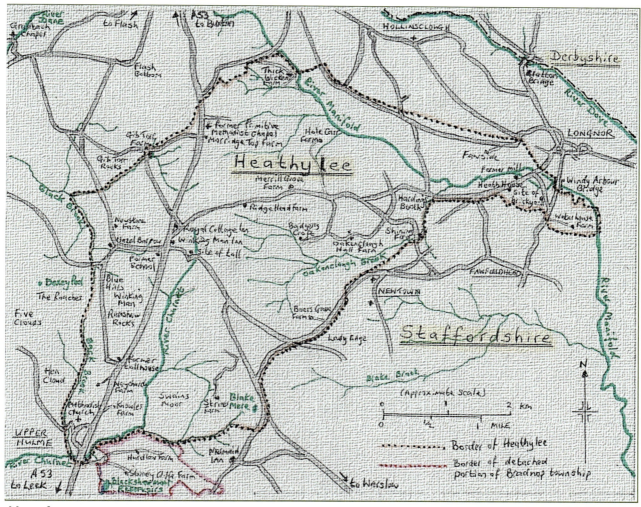

Map of Heathylee township.

The earliest settlement in 'Heathylee' township was at Upper Hulme, which was recorded as part of 'Leekfrith' township in the mid-13th century. There was an estate called 'Broncott' that was recorded on the Heathylee side of Back Brook in 1299, the name of which is derived from words meaning 'broom' and 'cottage'. There was a house called 'Naychurch', just north of Upper Hulme, recorded in the early 15th century, but earlier, to the east, there was a house on the site where 'Knowles' farm stands in 1308, and the tenant was recorded as Robert of Knolles. Further east, across what is known as Swains Moor, there was a house called 'Strines' by 1415, and there was a house at the site of Little Swainsmoor Farm in the early 16th century.

Further settlements began in the township, when Hardings Booth hamlet started developing about 1327 at the confluence of Oakenclough Brook and the River Manifold. The site of Oakenclough Hall was inhabited from the early 15th century, and a new house built there in 1747 was regarded as a 'hall', but this was replaced by farm buildings in the late 1890's. Even earlier was a house further upstream on Oakenclough Brook, known as Badgers Croft. This was recorded in 1308 as having a tenant by the name of Robert of Bochardescroft.

There was a house called 'Heathylee' recorded in 1406. This was thought to be situated to the north west of Hardings Booth, near to the River Manifold where a house called Hole Carr was recorded in 1414, and a house called Ball Bank was recorded in 1444. There was also another house called Heathylee recorded in 1571.

Coal Mining in Heathylee

The last area to be settled in the township was north of Ramshaw Rocks, in an area known as 'Blue Hills', which was so called because of coal deposits in the area causing the streams to be slightly blue in colour. Coal was being mined in the early 15th century when in 1401, a Richard Strongarme was given a year's long lease for two coal mines and a forge at Back Brook. Also, in the same year, a Thomas Smyth was given a year's lease to work a vein of coal at Black Brook. In 1404, a smithy named John Toples took a lease for life to work a vein of 140 feet of coal, also at Black Brook, but it seems he only worked the mine for three years.

In 1764, the new land owner, Sir Henry Harpur, gave a lease for a mine at Blue Hills for a period of 21 years to James and Tobias Mallors, with a rent of one tenth of the coal being excavated. In 1796, there was a 'Bluehills Colliery', which was then owned by the Earl of Macclesfield. The coal mining in the township was declining by this time, with limited resources and cheaper competition elsewhere meaning that by 1881, there was only one coal miner recorded in the census as living in the Blue Hills area, near to the Winking Man rock formations.

Other Industries in Heathylee

A house built in Upper Hulme in the late 18th century was known to be inhabited by a Joseph Billing, who was recorded as a quarryman and stone cutter. The house became an inn, known as the New Inn in the 1820's. It is still an inn today, and since 1994 has been known as 'The Olde Rock Inn'.

Several small quarries were opened later in the early 19th century along the road to Longnor. There were three stonemasons and three stone breakers listed in the census of 1861, by which time there was also a brickyard near to Longnor village, on the road before Longnor Bridge.

In 1404, near to Longnor Bridge, on the River Manifold, there was a mill called 'Frith Mill'. In 1605, Sir John Harpur replaced another nearby mill called 'Longnor Mill'. This was itself rebuilt in 1770 by a corn dealer named Richard Gould, of Brownhill. However, Gould became bankrupt in 1773, and the mill became disused. Longnor Mill re-opened in 1831, when it was enlarged to include a bone mill. The mill was also used to grind corn, until 1870 at least. The bone mill operations continued until 1890, and six years earlier, in 1884, part of the mill had started being used as a saw mill, specializing in the manufacture of 'rakes'. It remained in operation as a saw mill until the mid-1980's, and now the building is used as a private residence.

Another source of employment in the township began in 1601. A button maker was listed as living at a house called 'Stonieway', near to Hardings Booth. In 1680, a stream in a mine at Blue Hills was used to dye moulds for buttons, presumably a blue dye. Many women and girls in the area were listed as employed in a button making industry. Six women were listed as button makers in Heathylee in the 1841 census, and this number rose to 38 in 1851, and 42 in the census of 1861 from a total population of only 504 inhabitants of Heathylee township. However, there was a sharp decline in the industry, and only five people were recorded as button makers in 1881.

More recently, the township has seen a concentration of employment in the agricultural industry, yet as early as 1341 there were 'open fields' recorded at the Broncott estate, near Upper Hulme. Most of the area then was either covered in forest, or moorland, or was common waste land. The waste land lay chiefly on Morridge, as it seems similar today, which covered about 940 acres of land in an 1839 survey. By 1988 there was over 2000 hectares, or about 800 acres, of farmland recorded in the now civil parish. There were about 2000 cattle recorded, with more than 5000 sheep and 2000 pigs, with one farm being recorded as specialized in pig 'fattening'. There are about 55 farms listed in the civil parish with most being smaller than 50 hectares, or 20 acres.

Religion and Schooling in Heathylee Township

In the townships of both Heathylee and Hollinsclough there were no churches for the inhabitants to attend any religious guidance services before 1744, and almost all of the people would have made their way to St. Bartholomew's church in Longnor village. St. Bartholomew's was first recorded in 1448, though it is thought to have been in existence since the 12th century. From 1744, some of the inhabitants of these townships, as well as those from 'Quarnford' township, could now attend the newly built St. Paul's church in Flash village. There are records from about 1900 until the late 1950's that show some mission services were held in a school room, at a building on the main Leek to Buxton road that is near opposite the site of the Winking Man inn.

A short distance from the Royal Cottage Inn, along the Longnor road, is a house known as Ridge Head, which was the home of Isaac Billing. In the late 18th century the house was used to hold Methodist society meetings, where 46 people attended in 1803.

In 1829, Wesleyan Methodist services were held at the house named Hole Carr, which as mentioned previously was built before 1414. Methodist services were also recorded at Upper Hulme in 1837, and in the 1851 census a congregation of 30 people were recorded there. Many other farmhouses and houses were used for non-conformist services in the area, including a Primitive Methodist chapel that opened in 1853 at 'Morridge End', near Ramshaw Rocks, but this was replaced by 1880 with a building at 'Morridge Top', which was closed in 1972 and is now nothing more than the barn outbuilding seen at Morridge Top Farm.

There were no schools in Heathylee township before 1819, but in the 1830's there were two schools attended by fee paying children. There was also a Sunday school, where 120 children attended who were taught for free. A school board was set up in 1880, and in 1884 another school was built on the main Leek to Buxton road, as mentioned earlier, which was used for some church mission services from 1900. The cost of running the school was paid for by Sir John Harpur Crewe initially, then in 1903 it was known as the 'Ramshaw Council School'. However, pupils were later transferred to other schools in Leek and the school house was closed in 1970, when it was sold to become a private house.

5.3 *Rock Hall Cottage and Doxey Pool

Rock Hall cottage can be found at the southern end of the Roaches escarpment, of which Ramshaw rocks and the 'Winking Man' are a part of, whilst the northern end of the ridge has the 'Hanging Stone' and 'Lud's Church' gorge. The cottage of Rock Hall was built as a hunting lodge by Sir Philip Lancaster Brocklehurst of Swythamley Hall, but an old story suggests the site was originally the location of a cave dwelling, also known as Rock Hall. The cave was then occupied by an old woman named Bess Bowyer, who had lived to be nearly 100 years old.

Rock Hall was a large natural cavern which had been created by rock falls, in a similar way to Lud's Church formation. Bess Bowyer had apparently separated the inside of the cave into two rooms, one as a living room, and the other as a bedroom. Both of the rooms had an icy cold stream running through them. Also, at the back of the bedroom it was rumoured Bess had a secret escape route which she would use to assist smugglers and army deserters.

It is also said that Bess had a daughter who lived with her, a young attractive girl shrouded in mystery, who had a fine singing voice which could be heard emanating from amongst the rocks. It is thought by some that the young daughter was the identity of the legend of the 'Mermaid of Doxey Pool', which lies nearby.

The 'mermaid' that was said to inhabit Doxey Pool, was also said to sing, and anyone hearing her song would be irresistibly drawn to its dark waters where they would disappear into the depths. One winter's morning, Bess Bowyer was reportedly seen in distress, as apparently some strange men had carried off with her daughter, never to be seen again. Not long after this Bess was found in her cave, having died from a broken heart.

Doxey Pool was said to have been linked to the nearby Blake Mere, which was also sometimes known as the 'Mermaid Pool', by an underground stream or channel. Like Blake Mere, which was also thought to be a bottomless pool, and home to a mythical mermaid, there is also the rumour that Doxey Pool would see birds fly around it rather than over it. Both lakelets are, rather strangely, thought to be hundreds of feet above the level of all the local springs and stream heads, which only adds to the strength of fanciful rumours.

There is another story however, from 1949, which is a description of events from a woman by the name of Mrs. Florence Pettit, who was visiting the area with a friend from Buxton, and who had decided to try to go for a swim in Doxey Pool. This is what she had later written : -

" – a great 'thing' rose up from the middle of the lake. It rose very quickly until it was 25 to 30 feet tall. Seeming to be part of the slimy weeds and the water, yet it had eyes, and those eyes were extremely malevolent. It pointed its long boney fingers menacingly at me so there was no mistaking its hostility. I stood staring at the undine, water spirit, naiad or whatever it was, while my heart raced. Its feet just touched the surface of the water, the weeds and the air, when I dared to look again, the creature was dissolving back into the elements from which it had formed".

This descriptive text upholds a name given for the 'mermaid' as 'Jenny Greenteeth', which is a generic name for a malignant water spirit said to live in small pools and who drown children and strengthens the reputation that she lures people into the pool to their deaths. Some believe that the tale stems from the pool edge being covered in green algae, which could cause people to slip and fall into the pool. The description may also suggest the identity of the 'mermaid' to be Bess Bowyer, who is desperately searching for her lost daughter, and seeking revenge on the men who stole her away.

Mary, the Maid of the Inn

In the south-eastern part of the township of Heathylee, near to the house named Strines, on the edge of Swains Moor, there is a small pool named 'Blake Mere', which has also been known as the 'Mermaid Pool'. A few hundred metres away, on the road up to Morridge, there is an inn called the 'Mermaid'. There were a lot of rumours about Blake Mere which included stories that it was a bottomless pool, and that cattle would not drink from it, and even birds were said to fly around it rather than over it. All these stories were dismissed as fanciful tales by a Robert Plot, who wrote as an 'antiquary', collecting old stories and legends, in 1680.

He also wrote about another story involving Mary, the serving girl and maid from the Mermaid Inn, which he actually believed to be true. The story involved the rescue of Mary, whose lover, Richard, was caught trying to drown her in Blake Mere. She had discovered that her lover was not only a robber, but also a murderer and she was nearly murdered herself. The 'discovery event' of her attempted drowning became the subject of a poem, written by Robert Southey in 1796, which has 21 stanzas, and was called, "Mary, the Maid of the Inn" – which I thought worthy of reading here : -

i)   *Who is she, the poor Maniac, whose wildly-fix'd eyes*
        Seem a heart overcharged to express?
        She weeps not, yet often and deeply she sighs,
        She never complains, but her silence implies
        The composure of settled distress.

ii)   *No aid, no compassion the Maniac will seek,*
        Cold and hunger awake not her care:
        Thro' her rags do the winds of the winter blow bleak
        On her poor withered bosom half bare, and her cheek
        Has the deathy pale hue of despair.

iii)   *Yet cheerful and happy, nor distant the day,*
        Poor Mary the Maniac has been;
        The Traveller remembers who journeyed this way
        No damsel so lovely, no damsel so gay
        As Mary the Maid of the Inn.

iv)   *Her cheerful address fill'd the guests with delight*
        As she welcomed them in with a smile:
        Her heart was a stranger to childish affright,
        And Mary would walk by the Abbey at night
        When the wind whistled down the dark aisle.

v)   *She loved, and young Richard had settled the day,*
        And she hoped to be happy for life;
        But Richard was idle and worthless, and they
        Who knew him would pity poor Mary and say
        That she was too good for his wife.

vi)   *'Twas in autumn, and stormy and dark was the night*
        And fast were the windows and door;
        Two guests sat enjoying the fire that burnt bright,
        And smoking in silence with tranquil delight
        They listen'd to hear the wind roar.

vii)   *"Tis pleasant," cried one, "seated by the fire side*
    "To hear the wind whistle without."
    "A fine night for the Abbey!" his comrade replied,
    "Methinks a man's courage would now be well tried
    "Who should wander the ruins about."

viii)   *"I myself, like a school-boy, should tremble to hear*
    "The hoarse ivy shake over my head;
    "And could fancy I saw, half persuaded by fear,
    "Some ugly old Abbot's white spirit appear,
    "For this wind might awaken the dead!"

ix)   *"I'll wager a dinner," the other one cried,*
    "That Mary would venture there now."
    "Then wager and lose!" with a sneer he replied,
    "I'll warrant she'd fancy a ghost by her side,
    "And faint if she saw a white cow."

x)   *"Will Mary this charge on her courage allow?"*
    His companion exclaim'd with a smile;
    "I shall win, for I know she will venture there now,
    "And earn a new bonnet by bringing a bough
    "From the elder that grows in the aisle."

xi)   *With fearless good humour did Mary comply,*
    And her way to the Abbey she bent;
    The night it was dark, and the wind it was high
    And as hollowly howling it swept thro' the sky
    She shiver'd with cold as she went.

xii)   *O'er the path so well known still proceeded the Maid*
    Where the Abbey rose dim on the sight,
    Thro' the gate-way she entered, she felt not afraid
    Yet the ruins were lonely and wild, and their shade
    Seem'd to deepen the gloom of the night.

xiii)   *All around her was silent, save when the rude blast*
    Howl'd dismally round the old pile;
    Over weed-cover'd fragments still fearless she past,
    And arrived in the innermost ruin at last
    Where the elder tree grew in the aisle.

xiv)   *Well-pleas'd did she reach it, and quickly drew near*
    And hastily gather'd the bough:
    When the sound of a voice seem'd to rise on her ear,
    She paus'd, and she listen'd, all eager to hear,
    Aud her heart panted fearfully now.

xv)   *The wind blew, the hoarse ivy shook over her head,*
    She listen'd, -- nought else could she hear.
    The wind ceas'd, her heart sunk in her bosom with dread
    For she heard in the ruins distinctly the tread
    Of footsteps approaching her near.

xvi)   *Behind a wide column half breathless with fear*
         She crept to conceal herself there:
         That instant the moon o'er a dark cloud shone clear,
         And she saw in the moonlight two ruffians appear
         And between them a corpse did they bear.

xvii)   *Then Mary could feel her heart-blood curdle cold!*
         Again the rough wind hurried by, —
         It blew off the hat of the one, and behold
         Even close to the feet of poor Mary it roll'd, —
         She felt, and expected to die.

xviii)   *"Curse the hat!" he exclaims. "Nay come on and first hide*
         "The dead body," his comrade replies.
         She beheld them in safety pass on by her side,
         She seizes the hat, fear her courage supplied,
         And fast thro' the Abbey she flies.

xix)   *She ran with wild speed, she rush'd in at the door,*
         She gazed horribly eager around,
         Then her limbs could support their faint burthen no more,
         And exhausted and breathless she sunk on the floor
         Unable to utter a sound.

xx)   *Ere yet her pale lips could the story impart,*
         For a moment the hat met her view; —
         Her eyes from that object convulsively start,
         For – oh God what cold horror then thrill'd thro' her heart,
         When the name of her Richard she knew!

xxi)   *Where the old Abbey stands, on the common hard by*
         His gibbet is now to be seen.
         Not far from the road it engages the eye,
         The Traveller beholds it, and thinks with a sigh
         Of poor Mary the Maid of the Inn.

Robert Southey (1796)

125

5.4 *The Roaches

The 'Roaches', is the name given to a ridge of coarse sandstone that is approximately ten kilometres long, that stretches from 'Axe Edge', north of Flash village in the north, to 'Hen Cloud' in the south near to Upper Hulme. The name of the area has been derived from the French words of 'les roches' meaning 'the rocks' and is made up of spectacular rock formations, including Ramshaw Rocks, the Winking Man, Valkyrie and Five Clouds. The ridge rises up to a height of approximately 505 metres, or 1657 feet, which is described as a gritstone escarpment that is a popular area for ramblers and rock climbers.

The geography of the area is formed from a thick bed of coarse sandstone, or 'gritstone', that was developed in the geological period known as the 'Namurian Age', part of the Carboniferous Age, between 326 and 313 million years ago. The coarse sandstone in the area has taken the name of 'Roaches Grit', which has numerous surface outcrops of rock formations occurring widely throughout the western part of the Peak District.

Amongst the prominent features in the area that are formed of Roaches Grit, there is 'Axe Edge' and 'Wolf Edge' near to Flash village, along with 'Lud's Church' chasm and the 'Hangingstone' near to Danebridge village. The notable 'Winking Man' rock formation, at the northern tip of the so-called Ramshaw Rocks occur in the south eastern part of the Roaches, whilst Five Clouds and Hen Cloud form the southern end. The Roaches has an east to west fault line running through it that slightly separates Hen Cloud and Five Clouds from the rest of the area. The fault line runs through a valley that contains Black Brook to the north and Back Brook to the south, which had previously formed the western boundary of the 'township' of Heathylee.

The 'Five Clouds' rock formations were formed from a thinner bed of similar sandstone, which is simply called 'Five Clouds Sandstone'. The sandstones are thought to be originated from sand sediments dropped by major rivers from the Peak District in the north, millions of years ago. Near to the top of the Five Clouds formations is the infamous Doxey Pool, measuring approximately 15 metres by 10 metres, that according to legendary tales is inhabited by the water spirit of a mermaid called Jenny Greenteeth, who was also known as the 'blue nymph'.

The Roaches Estate was purchased by the 'Peak District National Park Authority in the 1980's to safeguard the area from any adverse developments. From 2013, the Staffordshire Wildlife Trust took on the management of the Roaches Estate, which is also an area that is thought to still being inhabited by a small colony of Australian Bennett wallabies, as released in the 1930's, as well as at least one pair of breeding peregrine falcons that have thrived in the steep rock faces since 2008.

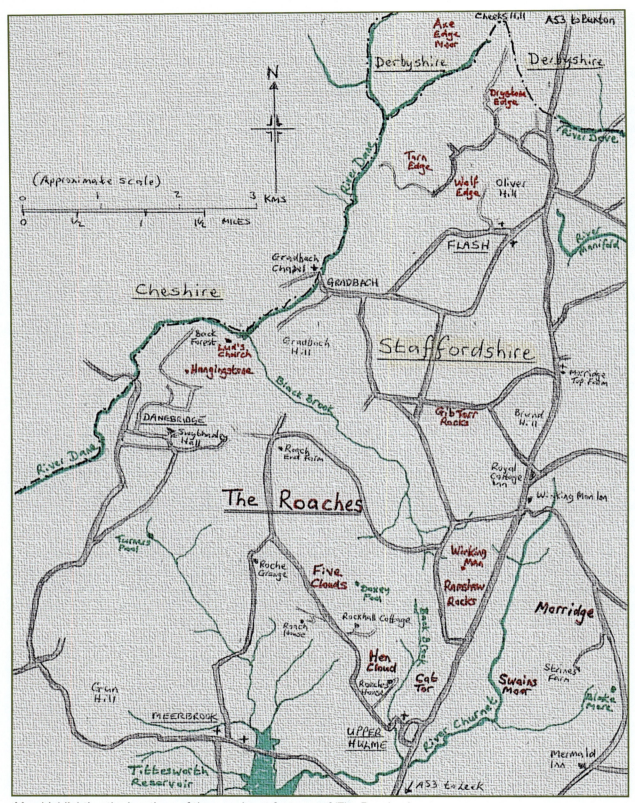

Map highlighting the locations of the prominent features of 'The Roaches'

Views of the 'Roaches' escarpment, as seen from the Mermaid Inn near Thorncliffe village

5.5 *Hollinsclough Township - A Brief History

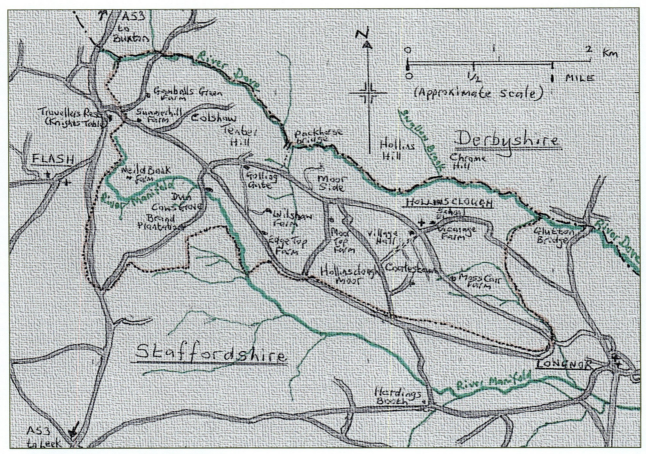

Township area of Hollinsclough

Hollinsclough 'township' was part of the 'Forest' tithing of Alstonefield manor in the late 1390's, which is when the village of Hollinsclough was first recorded. It was actually recorded as the village of 'Howelsclough' then. The village is situated in a small ravine formed by a stream which flows into the River Dove. The Old English word of 'hol', meaning 'hollow', and 'clough' or 'cloh' meaning steep 'valley' or ravine, were combined to make the name of the village. The name of Hollinsclough was used from around the late 1700's.

In 1594, the township shared a 'frankpledge' with the township of Heathylee – and the joint tithing was sometimes mentioned as 'High Frith'. This arrangement was still in place in 1676, but by 1697 Hollinsclough had its own frankpledge, and also had a nominated 'headborough'.

In the 1630's, the village only comprised of three houses and seven cottages, and later an inn was built, but this was closed in 1785. The population of the township was recorded at the 'manor court', and in 1769 there were 115 inhabitants in the township. By 1801 the population reached 562, and a high of 564 in 1831 before a decline in numbers began. There were 393 inhabitants in 1851, then 229 in 1901, and only 161 people recorded in 1991.

A number of settlements developed in the township area, including that of Colshaw, which had a number of buildings spread over an area of developing farmland. Summerhill, is a house that is dated 1757, and was built for a John Gaunt, who was recorded as a button merchant. Further along the road are Nether Colshaw Farm, Golling Gate, and Tenterhill Farm. A little further south is Edge Top Farm, which was built in 1787 for a Micah Mellor, who was recorded as a 'hawker'. Hawkers and 'pedlars' were people involved in the selling of inexpensive merchandise that could be easily transported around. Items generally included foodstuffs and handicrafts wares, with the area becoming renowned for its button industry and button merchants. The improving roads system in the area made this an easier task and some people thrived.

Two surveyors of the highways were appointed in Hollinsclough township by the manor court as early as 1601, and improvements to the roads were ongoing. The village itself became routed on a main road between Flash and Longnor, which was toll gated at Flash Bar. A more direct route was laid out however in 1843-4, which by-passed the village of Hollinsclough, so as to avoid the steep incline into the village. The new route ran on higher ground through an area called Coatestown, and up to Colshaw, passing Edge Top Farm. Coatestown was so called simply because there was a house for almost every member of a family named 'Coates', the first of which was Isaac Coates, who was recorded as a 'dealer' in the late 1750's.

The township's western boundary runs from just north of the Morridge Top farm, where an old Methodist chapel once stood, up to the Derbyshire border at Dove Head farm. To the west lies the township of Quarnford which has been detailed previously, and which also includes the source of the River Manifold. The River Manifold is a key landmark in the township of Hollinsclough, as is the River Dove which forms the entire northern boundary.

The name of 'Dove' is thought to have been derived from an old 'Britannic' word of 'dubo', which meant black or dark. So, the River Dove was known as the 'dark river' and was supposedly a reference from the upper reaches of the Dove valley, presumably linked to the sources of coal that were found there and the colouring of the streams in the area with a black or blue tinge. This was the same reason there was an area called 'Blue Hills' in the Heathylee township as previously outlined.

The name of the 'Manifold' river is a little more straightforward, in that its name relates to the many turns or 'folds' in its twelve-mile course. The river was recorded in 1434 with the name of "Water of Manifould".

The township has its highest point near this western boundary, where the building now known as Summerhill farm stands at 1513 feet (or 461 metres) above sea level. There is a ridge between the River Dove and the River Manifold that tapers downhill from the Dove Head, and source of the Manifold, to an area near Glutton Bridge on the River Dove near Longnor at 883 feet (or 269 metres). In between, spanning the River Dove near Tenterhill farm, there is a small packhorse bridge, still intact today, at the confluence of a small stream that runs down from Tenter Hill to a place known as 'Washgate'. This is thought to be because of the washing of fleeces and sheep taking place in the river there. There was mention of another packhorse bridge near to Hollinsclough village further downstream, but this is not there today.

Hollinsclough Industries – 'Breeches, Waistcoats, and Tenter Hooks'

There was a fulling mill recorded just a little north-west above the village of Hollinsclough, on the River Dove, when cloth working took place in the area as early as 1564. In an area known previously as 'Gollin', where Golling Gate and Tenterhill farms are today, there was a small community of hand weavers of silk. In the 1851 census there were 19 silk weavers listed in just 13 houses in the area. The area called Tenter Hill has two fields which were named 'Breeches' and 'Waistcoat', where there were some remains of what was once thought to be the site of the fulling mill.

After cloth was 'fulled', it was taken from the mill to be dried. This was done on a wooden frame work, which were called 'tenter frames', so the name of Tenter Hill was taken from this process. The 'tenting' frames consisted of upright wooden posts, with a fixed top rail and a bottom rail which was adjusted by pegs and wedges. Both rails were fitted every two or three inches along with 'tenter hooks', which were 'L' shaped double pointed clouts or nails. The hooks in the top rail pointed upwards, and the bottom hooks pointed down. The wet cloth was hooked by its edges to both rails with the lower rail adjusted to make the cloth tight to the frame, and then cut to an even width.

By the mid-18th century the phrase 'on tenterhooks' came into being, which had the meaning of "being in a state of tension, uneasiness, or suspense". Figuratively it meant, 'stretched like the cloth on the tenter frame'.

The township has had a history of agricultural use since an open field, called 'Town Field', was recorded in 1617. This field comprised of an area of approximately 11 acres of arable land, with an extra 8 ½ acres used as a cornfield. The field is thought to be located just past the new primary school on the right-hand side of the road and was still being used in 1725 as Town Field. By 1988, farmland accounted for nearly 650 acres of the total land area of the township, which was measured at 1,842 acres. The farmland was divided into a total of 24 farms, all of varying sizes, which held over 800 cattle and 1300 sheep.

A successful industry that thrived in the township, along with Quarnford township, was that of the button making industry. Numerous button merchants were recorded in the area, including a William Wood, who was living in Hollinsclough c.1757-1769, and an Ezekiel Wood, maybe related, living in Colshaw as a button maker in 1764. John Gaunt, as mentioned earlier, had a house built in 1757 at Summerhill, was also recorded as a button merchant in 1764. He was so successful at his trade that by 1772 he was known locally as 'the King of Flash', which was a reference to Flash village being the centre of the button making trade.

Obadiah Tunnicliffe, who lived at Colshaw in 1769, was described as a button manufacturer working in Flash in 1787. His son, Moses Tunnicliffe, continued working in the trade, and by 1820 he had a warehouse and a factory in Macclesfield. The button making industry was still flourishing over the next forty years, with 21 button makers recorded in the township of Hollinsclough in the 1861 census.

Hawkers and pedlars were recorded in Hollinsclough township as early as 1600. The afore-mentioned Isaac Coates was a dealer in the late 1750's. At first, he bought and sold goods from travellers to sell on to the local inhabitants, and then from 1770 he bought goods directly from manufacturers in Manchester. At that time, he had three men employed by him to sell his wares, but this was to be a short-lived venture because by 1774 he was declared bankrupt.

John Lomas, who was the son of a pedlar named George Lomas, became a hawker himself in 1764 then later became a wholesale dealer like Isaac Coates. As previously mentioned, he moved to Hollinsclough village in 1785, and was involved in the petition presented to the government regarding licences for hawking. Perhaps more importantly, he became involved in the Methodist movement and local religious guidance, so much so that he built the village chapel, and his story is worthy of a separate section below.

5.6 *John Lomas (1747 – 1823)

In the 18th century, many cottagers around Flash village, and in the High Frith townships, worked as pedlars and hawkers. In the ancient parish of Alstonefield there were approximately 400 hawkers and pedlars recorded in 1785. It was in that year that the government had drawn up plans to abolish licenses for the trade of hawkers, and it prompted a reaction from those in the trade to set up a petition to take to the House of Commons.

John Lomas of Hollinsclough was a member of a delegation of hawkers from the north – west of England which had an audience with the prime minister, William Pitt, in an effort to put forward a case for continuing with the current licensing arrangement for hawkers. They argued, as it was stated later, that 'hawkers in Alstonefield ancient parish had converted a barren and wild spot to a rich and fertile circuit'. They had their views upheld and were successful in maintaining their licences.

John Lomas was born at Colshaw, in Hollinsclough township, in 1747. He was the son of George Lomas, a local pedlar, and as a small child he travelled around with his father, no doubt picking up tips of the trade of hawking. When he became 16 years old, his father entrusted him with a pack of goods, and bought him his own licence to trade. He gradually built up a successful business, and by 1785 when he moved to Hollinsclough village, he had ten men working for him. His successful trip to the House of Commons to preserve his licence meant that he could continue his successful business ventures.

He was married in 1768, at the age of 21, to a woman called Sarah. In 1783 they had listened to the preaching of John Wesley, most probably at Longnor, and had decided to become committed Christians. In 1797, John Lomas decided to use his wealth from the hawker trade to build his own chapel in his garden. This Methodist chapel was opened on Easter Day, 1801. It had cost approximately £355 to build, as this had actually been rebuilt after an original building on the site was used for meetings of the Methodist society from 1786.

John Lomas, and his family before him, had links to the local lords of the manor, the Harpur, Crewe, and Harpur-Crewe family that held the land and title for 350 years. In 1820, John Lomas was asked to write a letter to Sir George Crewe to detail events that had occurred on his visit to the Houses of Parliament in 1785, along with details about how he grew his business and of his parentage. Some extracts from this letter made interesting reading :-

"To the Honourable Sir Geo. Crewe Baron. Dear Sir, in obedience to your request I set down to give you a short, and to the best of my knowledge, a true account of my parentage –
About 80 or 90 years back, my Great Granfather, Geo. Lomas, served as Gamekeeper to Sir John Harpur, your great Granfather. G.Lomas, the Venerable old keeper, had by his wife Dinah, 4 children. Namely John, Sarah, Ellen, and Micah. GL, lived I was told, to the age of 102...... My old Unkle John succeeded his father as gamekeeper....".

"My Granfather, Micah, died aged about 95. My father GL died aged 85, about 15 years back.......... and now honoured Sir, with regard to myself, my Father and Mother, Geo. and Ann Lomas were poor pedlars who took me to travel before I was 8 years old, to which I submitted, with all its toils, hardships and wants, until I arrived at the age of 16".

"My Mother died when I was about 12, and my Father Married a second wife, and had many children......... I began in the world for myself and the blessing of the Lord accompanying my hard labour and steady frugality. I soon saved money to buy a pack of goods of my own; when the Gentlemen of Manchester and other places offered me credit. With this I steadily endeavoured to pay my creditors and please my customers and my profits increased until I had 10 men travelling under me".

"Our country were much Alarmed to hear the Hawkers & Pedlars were to be abolished, the Shop Tax Bill being passed, the Pedlars Act must be repealed & that body of people Prohibited from carrying on their business: June 2nd – my wife had been delivered of a son and at night I was called to Attend a Meeting of our Travellers & Tradesmen from Manchester when it was deemed Immediately Necessary to Petition Parlament"....

"...and so must be brief – the next sitting the Shop tax being repealed. We again petitioned against the Double Duty and the restrictions and got them all taken off so that the Hawkers Act is better than it was a century back; praise the lord."

"And now Honoured Sir, you having droped a word in my hearing when on the road the other day struck my mind whith hope and pleasure; when I heard you say you was but Steward under God true Hord Sir, we are all Stewards and everyone has a tallant to improve – some have many!! Lord give grace to improve them".

"Yet he that cometh yo god as a penitent and true believer trusting in the merits and death of Christ alone, may be saved without one scrap of his own righteous ness had this been the case I had as a chief sinner, been lost for Ever!"

"Pray pardon the liberty I have taken in these last lines, I daren't say more for fear of giving offence; and therefore beg leave to subscribe my self ..... Honor'd Sir......Yours most Truly ....

John Lomas
Hollinsclough, 11th August 1820."

Religious Following In Hollinsclough Township

It is easy to see from the letter above how John Lomas became a committed Christian, and in 1786 when he held Methodist meetings, he had a 'society' of followers, though only 11 members to begin with. The Chapel he started to build later was registered for Methodist meetings in 1797, with himself as the minister, and Sunday services were held fortnightly in 1798, on alternate Sundays to the chapel in Longnor. His society had 23 members in 1803.

Before the late 17th century, the nearest church to offer any religious guidance was at Longnor' St. Bartholomew's Church. From 1744, those living in the western part of Hollinsclough township could attend the newly built St. Paul's church in Flash village, and in 1902 the western area of Hollinsclough was assigned to the Quarnford parish.

In 1840, Sir George Crewe, prompted by the curate of Longnor church – William Buckwell, decided to have a barn rebuilt in Hollinsclough village, so as to provide another church and a Sunday school there. He also converted a farmhouse into a house for a new curate to live in. This was sited next door to John Lomas's Methodist chapel, and I wonder what his feelings would have been had he been alive, as John Lomas had died in 1823.

The church was licensed in 1841 and was called St. Agnes Church in 1906. The first curate was a Henry Smith, who was paid £50 by Sir George Crewe. However, he left his post in 1846, and the church of St. Agnes was served by the curate of Quarnford. The curate started living in Hollinsclough village as the vicarage house in Flash was in a poor condition. Regular services were last held there in 1956, and the church was closed in 1966, becoming a residential field centre.

John Lomas died in 1823, but he left instructions that a manuscript should be published and given to every household in Hollinsclough village, along with those within a mile from it. The manuscript was entitled – "The Last Legacy of John Lomas to the people of Hollinsclough and its Vicinity". The chapel he built was still open in 1994, and is still there today as a listed building, but intriguingly as a "Bethel" chapel. I was interested to know why and what was a Bethel chapel so the following section enlightened me.

Hollinsclough Methodist "Bethel" Chapel, opened in 1801.

5.7 *Bethel and 'Jacob's Ladder'

The origins of the word 'Bethel' are found in many forms in various Bibles, but the earliest mention of Bethel refers to a settlement in Israel (possibly as early as 930 BC and before 721 BC). Bethel was an important religious centre for the northern Kingdom of Israel, following the break-up of a once united kingdom of David and Solomon.

The second 'Book of Kings' in the Bible describes Jeroboam, the first King of Israel (c.930BC-901BC), setting up two centres for so-called 'Golden Calf' worship. One centre was at a place called Dan, and the other was at Bethel, but Jeroboam's decision to shun Mushite priests at Shiloh, which was the original religious centre for Israel at the time, deeply offended the Shiloh priesthood and caused a lot of animosity towards Jeroboam.

Bethel had escaped destruction in 721 BC when Assyrians were conquering Israel, but it was later occupied by King Joshua of Judah (c.640-609 BC), who almost destroyed the ancient Israelite religious centre. Bethel then became inhabited again, and was "fortified by Bacchides the Syrian, in the time of the Maccabees". However, later transcripts refer to Bethel being captured by Vespasian, who was Roman Emperor from AD69 to AD79, and writings by Saint Jerome before AD 420 are the last known references to Bethel's existence.

Bethel, in 'Ugaritic' form, was known as Bt il, meaning 'House of El' or 'House of God', and in Hebrew it was known as Beth El, or Beth-El, and Beit El. In the Hebrew Bible it was described as being located between Benjamin and Ephraim. During Israelite rule, Bethel first belonged to the 'Tribe of Benjamin', but was later conquered by the 'Tribe of Ephraim'. Saint Jerome had described it as a small village that lay 12 Roman miles north of Jerusalem.

Bethel is mentioned several times in the Book of Genesis. It is in Genesis 28, when Jacob is fleeing from the wrath of his brother Esau, and Jacob falls asleep on a stone and dreams of a ladder, stretching between Heaven and Earth, thronged with angels. God stands at the top of the ladder and promises Jacob that he shall have the land of Canaan. When Jacob awakens he anoints the stone on which he has been sleeping, which is referred to as 'baetylus', and names, or renames the place there as 'Bethel'. Another account from Genesis 35 gives the name of El-Bethel, but both versions state that the original name for the place of his sleep was actually 'Luz', in Canaan.

When Jacob awoke from his dream, it is written in Genesis that he spoke the words – "Surely the Lord is in this place, ... this is none other than the house of God, and this is the gate of Heaven". After this he names the place as Bethel, the House of God, and the interpretations that followed of Jacobs Ladder being the 'Stairway to Heaven' have evolved into places of worship being called Bethel chapels, such as the John Lomas built chapel in Hollinsclough, and gives the thought that following a path of belief will show you the pathway to Heaven.

5.8 *Education in Hollinsclough

In 1799, the inhabitants of Hollinsclough nominated the well-known John Lomas to become the master of a school in the township. The school is thought to have been established by John Bourne of Newcastle-under-Lyme, who was also the benefactor of a school built in Flash village in 1760. John Bourne was also described as 'a considerable benefactor to the school at Colshaw', which was situated near to Summerhill, and also near to where John Lomas was born in 1747.

There was a Methodist Sunday school open in 1811, which was attended in 1830 by 32 boys and 38 girls. In 1840 part of the chapel built by John Lomas was used as a schoolhouse. In 1873, a separate schoolroom was built on the west side of the chapel and was to become known as the 'Hollinsclough Church of England School'. This was an all-age school until the 1940's when older pupils were transferred to schools in Leek.

In January 1960, a new school building was opened, next to the former St. Agnes Church which was closed in 1966. Only 25 children were in attendance, with the local population beginning to dwindle. The school eventually became 'grant maintained' in the early 1990's, then on 1st September 1999 it became the 'Hollinsclough C of E (Voluntary Aided) Primary School'. In a bid to ensure the school having a viable future, the principal, Mrs. Janette Mountford-Lees took the bold step to introduce a 'Flexi-school' concept, which boosted the school attendance from a mere 5 pupils in 2009 to over 50 in 2015. On 1st September 2015, the school became the 'Hollinsclough C of E Academy', joining forces with the Bursley Academy and the Manifold Primary to form the 'Bursley Multi-Academy Trust'.

Flexi – Schooling

Mrs. Janette Mountford-Lees adopted the 'Flexi-school' concept following guidelines that were set out in a 2007 Department of Education document. The 'Elective Home Education Guidelines for Local Authorities (England) 2007, Subsection 5.6' states –
" 'Flexi-schooling', or 'flexible school attendance', is an arrangement, between the parent and the school where the child is registered, to attend the school on a part time basis. The rest of the time the child is home educated (on authorised absence from school). This can be either on a long-term basis, or as a short term measure for a particular reason. 'Flexi-schooling' is a legal option provided that the head teacher of the school concerned agrees to the arrangement. The child will be required to follow the National Curriculum whilst at school".

At present, Hollinsclough Academy is adopting a policy which means that pupils are required to attend for three 'Core Days' of education, currently Tuesday, Wednesday, and Thursday. The Flexi-school policies and methodologies are designed and implemented taking into account the guidelines set out in the UNESCO approach to education, which are summarised with the '4 A's'. These are labelled as, Availability, Accessibility, Acceptability, and Adaptability, the framework for which was developed by a UN Special Rapporteur on the Right for Education, a Katarina Tomasevski.

Availability : implies that good quality education must be made available to all by eliminating barriers, be they financial, physical, or institutional/systemic.
Accessibility : implies that the 'available' education must also be made accessible to all, by eliminating all forms of discrimination and through installing flexible modes of education, particularly for the most vulnerable and marginalised who may not be reached otherwise by conventional modes.
Acceptability : implies further steps to make learning opportunities acceptable in terms of quality and relevance to the learners experiences and environment. This means ensuring that the education meets the minimum standards set by governments.
Adaptability : implies that education programmes must be adaptable to the various needs of the learners, rather than the learners adapting to fit in to a prescribed system, especially with regard to marginalised and vulnerable children.

5.9 *Fawfieldhead Township - A Brief History

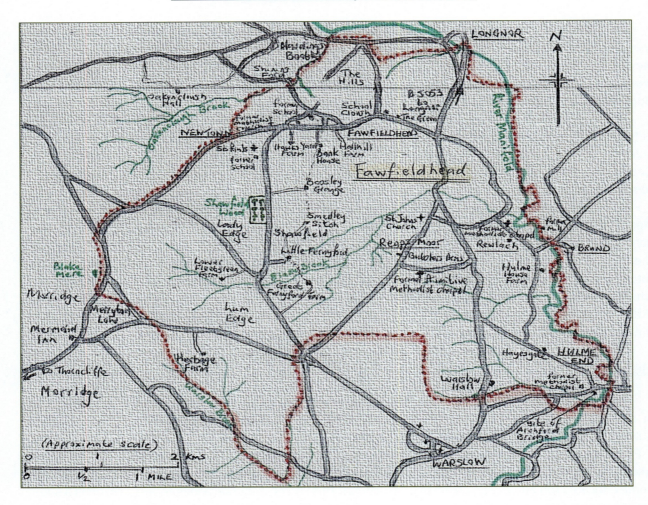

Fawfieldhead township was named after an area of land called 'Fawfield', which was recorded in 1308 as an area between the valley of Blake Brook and Oakenclough Brook. The name originates from words meaning 'multi-coloured open land' and may have referred to a range of many different coloured wild flowers in the area. The earliest settlements in the township area are thought to be at 'School Clough', where a house was recorded in 1331, and a little south from there the site of 'Smedley Sytch' was occupied in 1406.

Fawfieldhead was part of the 'forest tithing' of Alstonefield parish in the 1390's, and by 1594 there were enough settlers to form its own 'tithing'. A 'tithing' was an ancient administrative unit usually consisting of ten family units, or ten men, who were held responsible for its member's good behaviour. Its activities were overseen by the 'manor court', which in this case would have been run by the Lords of Alstonefield, but Longnor, not Alstonefield, had become the main settlement in the ancient parish.

There are four smaller main settlements in the township of Fawfieldhead, with Hulme End in the south eastern corner, and Newtown in the north western area. Fawfieldhead hamlet itself is in the north, and east of centre is Reaps Moor. Some scattered houses in the township included a house at Boosley Grange, which has some original 17th century stonework and was built for the Wardle family in the 1640's. Further north is Bank House, and on the boundary is Shining Ford, where a small hamlet existed in the 1630's. The hamlet once had a road connecting from there, through to Smedley Sytch, via Bank House and Boosley Grange.

In the 1630's, the hamlet of Fawfieldhead was known as 'Fawfieldgreen'. The population of the township grew slowly, with limited job opportunities and a large area of waste land gradually being converted to farm land, when the manor court in 1769 recorded only 143 inhabitants. This rose to a peak in 1821 of 1,315 inhabitants, and although efforts by the land-owning family, the Harpur-Crewe's, to increase settlement by building more churches and encouraging farming, there was a decline in population of the township, so that by 1991 only 300 people were recorded as living there.

A house on the west side of the hamlet of Fawfieldhead is dated 1774, which was extended in 1831 for an Isaac Billing, who was recorded as a stonemason in 1834. There was also a stonemason recorded in 1813 named Simon Billing, though it is not sure if they were related. Stone masons and stone workers were living in the township in relatively large numbers, as in the 1841 census there were 28 people recorded as being involved in the industry. In the 1851 census there is also a John Lomas recorded as a stonemason/brick and tile maker at Reaps Moor, who had 30 men working for him. This is obviously not John Lomas the minister at Hollinsclough Methodist church, who died in 1823, but he may have been a descendant or relative.

The total land area of the township is approximately 4,600 acres, with the highest point being at 1,588 feet (474 metres) above sea level near to the western boundary at Merryton Low. The lowest point is in the Manifold valley at the eastern corner at Hulme End, which lies at about 700 feet (213 metres) above sea level. In between, running through the middle of the township, is Blake Brook and its tributary streams that flow into the River Manifold east of Reaps Moor, near a house named Rewlach. A former Methodist church and a former mill stood near the confluence of Blake Brook and the Manifold. The mill was run by a John Shirley from Rewlach in the 1820's, but this was closed down by 1908.

The area known as Fawfield, as recorded in 1308, had a dairy farm recorded at the same date. The area had 'pasture rights' for about 300 acres of land to the north, at the area known as 'The Fawfield Hills'. However, these pasture rights were given by the Lords of Alstonefield, who had decided to try to encourage more settlement of the township by dividing the pasture into 'strips' for tenants of their land. This was complicated by the fact that inhabitants of Longnor also had pasture rights to 'The Fawfield Hills', and in 1568 there was an incident where 100 Longnor men were involved in tearing down fences that had been erected on the pasture strips by Fawfieldhead inhabitants. As a result, a few years later in 1575, it was stipulated that part of 'The Fawfield Hills', nearest to Longnor village, would be 'inclosed land' to be used only by Longnor inhabitants. However, this was further complicated when it was revealed that even this area would be shared with four farms in Heathylee township whose land border was partly included in the 'inclosed land'.

Nearby, on the outskirts of Newtown, there was a heath land area called 'Lady Edge', which extended northwards into Heathylee township. This area was also 'inclosed' after an Act of Paliament in 1834 and came under the ownership of the Lord of the Manor, Sir George Crewe. It was Sir George who instructed trees to be planted to form Shawfield Wood, on what was formerly waste land.

Newtown existed in 1754 as a 'hamlet' on the edge of common waste land. In 1836, Sir George Crewe was visiting the area and considered it to be a suitable site for further development, and so, encouraged by the curate of Longnor, had a church built in 1837. This was named in 1910 as St. Paul's, but despite the building of the church to encourage more settlers, the village remained a small concern. However, in a similar situation at Reaps Moor 'hamlet', where Sir George had a church built in 1842 and which was named St. John's in 1910, there was slightly more success with the influx of stone masons and stone workers flocking to the village. Settlement was made easier by the fact that they had the skills to build more houses using the local stone sources.

Religion and Education in Fawfieldhead Township

Most inhabitants of the township of Fawfieldhead attended religious guidance at the church of St. Bartholomew in Longnor village, where the church was first recorded in 1448 but was thought to have a Norman font which could have been there as early as the 12th century. New churches, though smaller in size, were built with the help of the Lord of Alstonefield, Sir George Crewe, after being prompted by the curate of Longnor church, William Buckwell. In 1837 a church was built in Newtown hamlet, and in 1842 a new church was built in Reaps Moor.

From the 1860's, the Harpur-Crewe family also provided a house near Fawfieldhead hamlet, called 'The Green', which was used by a curate to serve both Newtown and Reaps Moor churches. The curate was also paid a generous £100 for his services by Sir John Harpur-Crewe who was now the head of the family and the estate linked to the Lords of Alstonefield baronetcy.

The church at Newtown was named St. Paul's in 1910, which had an extension of a south west porch added to it in 1891. Earlier, Sir George Crewe had installed a bell and a table for psalm singers, two years before his death in 1844. The psalm singers lead the services in the church until 1861 when a harmonium was installed, at the same time that a harmonium was installed into the church at Reaps Moor.

The church at Reaps Moor was named St. John's in 1910 and was actually only part of a former workhouse. It held services on the upper floor, and on the Sunday service of census Sunday of 1851 there was an evening attendance of 65 adults. Earlier in the afternoon, a service at the Newtown church recorded an attendance of 64 people.

Methodist Followers in Fawfieldhead

A farmhouse at Smedley Sytch was thought to have been used as a meeting place for a Methodist society, which was recorded in 1765 at 'Sytch'. The society had 13 members in 1784.

In 1798 a monthly Methodist meeting was recorded at School Clough in the hamlet of Fawfieldhead, and near to Reaps Moor a Wesleyan Methodist society was recorded in 1837, having 27 members. A Methodist chapel was built there in 1849, near a house called 'Rewlach', where the occupant Mary Shirley had become a Methodist follower after hearing a preacher in Longnor market place in 1785.

The chapel near Rewlach had a recorded attendance of 70 people on census Sunday of 1851, which was a larger attendance than those at the conformist churches of Newtown and Reaps Moor. This serves to reiterate an observation noted earlier that the Methodist movement had a strong influence in the region, with societies and meetings formed in Danebridge, Gradbach, Flash, and Rushton Spencer. There was also a small Methodist society that had formed in Newtown, with 12 members recorded in 1810. A Wesleyan Methodist chapel was built less than 400 metres from St. Paul's church in 1841, only four years after the church had been built itself, and at the 1851 census Sunday evening service there were 41 people recorded. The chapel was however closed in 1975 and converted into the house there today.

Education in Fawfieldhead

There were no schools recorded in the township of Fawfieldhead in 1819, but in the early 1830's there were three 'day schools'. These had an attendance of 24 boys and 21 girls, who were paying fees to attend. There was also a Sunday school recorded with 54 boys and 56 girls attending. One of the three fee paying schools was to the west of Fawfieldhead hamlet, on the road to Newtown, which is now converted into the house as seen below.

Former fee-paying school house near Fawfieldhead/Newtown

In 1841, a Sunday school was recorded in Newtown village itself, initially being held in the church that had recently been built and supported by Sir George Crewe. In 1880, the school moved to a new building a few yards south along the road, becoming the Newtown Church of England School, which was funded by a committee of rate payers. In the 1930's, the school had 37 all–aged children attending, but a decision was made to transfer senior children to schools in Leek, as had other schools in Leek parish townships, leaving the Newtown school as a junior school. However, this was closed down in 1964, and the children were transferred to Longnor primary school.

DISCOVERING STAFFORDSHIRE

An Historical Companion Guide

To Walking In North Staffordshire

Longnor Village

(Walk No. GM06   —   August)

The main focus for this walk was to get a feeling for an old village in Staffordshire and to find as many of the thirty-two 'listed buildings/structures' in the village area of Longnor that I could. The listed structures range from bridges, farmhouses and cottages, to pubs and even a mile post. Many of these can be found in the village of Longnor itself, but a few were found within a few miles walking distance which added a little scenic viewing to the walk, as well as a little healthy exercise and some muddy boots.

As a starting point, thinking it might be interesting to view, I drove to the mysterious 'listed' mile post and found a small lay-by to park up that was close to it. I was a little disappointed to find a small, 18 inches high, triangular shaped white painted roadside post, which did not seem to warrant such an important 'listing', especially in comparison to the more impressive St. Bartholomew' Church in the village centre.

The listed bridges, which include Glutton Bridge, Longnor Bridge and Windy Arbour Bridge were also pretty average viewing. After a short uphill walk back to the mile post and continuing on the road back towards Longnor, I was then faced with a muddy trek near to Gauledge Farm. I was beginning to think I had a disappointing walk set up. However, things were about to change as I approached the village of Longnor, walking along Gauledge Lane. There are about five or six listed buildings here, all with different characteristics, with West Bank House and Sheffield House among them.

I decided to walk slightly out of the village from here, heading towards the Longnor Saw Mill, near Longnor Bridge. This was mentioned in my previous walk, which is in the extreme corner of Heathylee township, and was built on a site that dates as far back as 1770 when a mill there was rebuilt with the funding from the Harpur family, the Lords of Alstonefield. Continuing the walk along the south of the village to see the other bridge in the area, known as Windy Arbour Bridge, a look back towards the village gave a nice view of the prominent tower of the church of St. Bartholomew.

The village itself is dominated by a small market square, which is taken up by a car park now and is surrounded by at least three listed 'inns', of which the Horseshoe Inn is the oldest. This has been used as a location scene in the TV series Peak Practice and seems appropriate as it is just actually in the Peak District. The more locally renowned Crewe and Harpur Arms catches the eye more, mainly for its archway that is the entrance to the old listed 'Coachmans House'.

A walk up to the High Street passes another pub, called the Cheshire Cheese, which reflects on a local cheese making industry near Glutton Bridge which stored its cheese near the pub as far back as 1464. Then I turned back into the village towards the church and found a few more interesting listed buildings, particularly with a row of houses in Queen Street, as well as a few cottages on Church Street, before the view of St. Bartholomew' Church. The church was rebuilt in the 18th century but is thought to be on foundations of a previous church from around the 12th century.

In some ways I found the last part of my walk around the village to be the most pleasing. The old Wesleyan Chapel, where John Wesley was reported to have preached, is among a group of fantastic old stone buildings in Chapel Street, where worn steps appear in a narrow, cobbled street walkway inviting you into the intimacy of the old village. Then back to the market square which was set up by Sir John Harpur, the father of the first baronet of Alstonefield, in 1595.

Finally, I walk back to the mile post, although it is actually only about half a mile from the village I thought, passing the school opposite St. Bartholomew' church and taking in the country air as I make my way back to the parking space. I stop then to ponder over my thoughts of what a village life may have been like over 500 years ago and consider whether today's quieter village life is any improvement on the past.

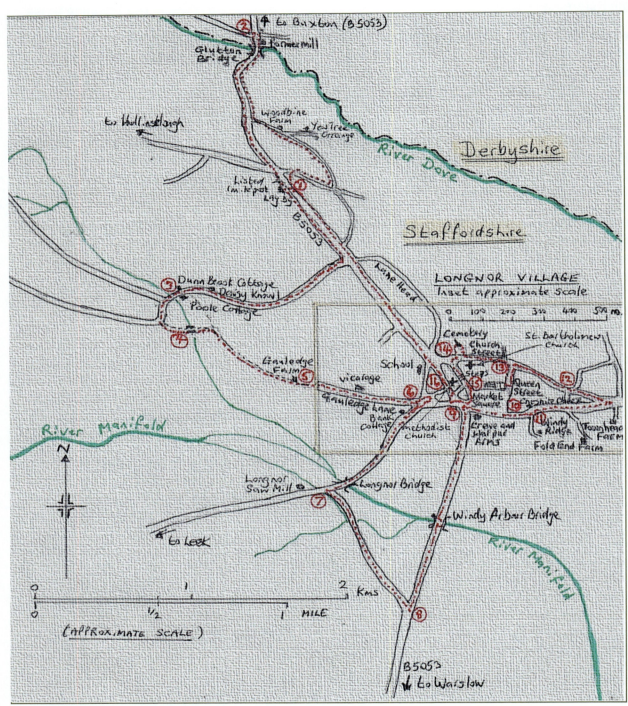

Walk GM06 – Longnor village

Walk Reference – GM06   Longnor Village

As with my previous walk, drive to the start point using the A53 Leek to Buxton Road and travelling from Leek you will soon come to the 'Winking Man' rock formation on your left, which is followed by the pub on the right, also called the Winking Man. Just past this, also on your right, is the Royal Cottage Inn, where a right turn is sign posted for Longnor. This road goes through the hamlet of Hardings Booth before coming into Longnor village. Turn left onto the B5053 Buxton road and then drive past the school on the left for half a mile to a small lay-by on the left, (Grid Ref. SK 08370 65617), which is just before a road that leads to Hollinsclough. Alternatively, there is the car park in the village market square.

<u>Walk Details</u>

The walk is about four and a half kilometres and takes about three and a half hours in total, which includes time to walk around the village at a leisurely pace. From the start point, there is a short trek into a depression which is called 'Under the Hill', which looks like a small river valley and is fairly near to the River Dove. Then a short walk along the Buxton road brings you to the Glutton Bridge, where there used to be a mill, and a cheese making industry. Walk back up the Buxton road for a mile, passing the start point, turning into another Hollinsclough road to the River Manifold. There is a short trek into a field, which is very boggy near the stream crossing, then uphill across fields to the edge of the Longnor village. Another section of roads follows this, over two bridges, then back into the village to explore the variety of listed buildings therein.

1) - Starting at the lay-by, which is near to the first listed structure, the 'Longnor half mile post', I cross over the road immediately opposite the lay-by, where a footpath post points down across the fields. However, it is much easier to walk down the concreted track which has a cattle grid to negotiate at first, and then go downhill for about 300 metres, when the track bends near to a house. Turn left into the field just before the house, then walk into the field there for about 50 metres before veering left, following the line of telephone wires and posts, which admittedly is not the most scenic of walks, but it leads to a farmhouse, which is Woodbine Farm.

At first, I thought this was the second listed building on my list, but I later found that I should have turned right at this farm and walked along the driveway to get to Yew Tree Grange Farmhouse, so alas I had missed one of my viewing points. Instead I found my way walking up a tarmac drive to meet up with the Buxton road, where a short way down the hill you can get a good view of Chrome Hill in Derbyshire.

'Listed' Longnor Mile Post

View of Chrome Hill, Derbyshire from the Buxton (B5053) road

2) – Walk down the Buxton road for another 400 metres and you will see the River Dove is crossed by Glutton Bridge. A house on the right used to be the mill, but it has been renovated, or rebuilt, over time so that it does not resemble a mill now, but there was a working mill at this site between 1820 and 1930. Glutton Bridge itself was rebuilt in the early 1820's following flood damage along with the other Longnor bridges.

*(Walk time – approx. 30 minutes)

Site of mill house at Glutton Bridge   Glutton Bridge, as rebuilt c.1822

3) – After viewing the bridge, head back up the Buxton road, passing the farm drive previously walked, and continue back to the mile post. Continue down the road towards Longnor village for about 300 metres past the car lay-by where a road runs off to the right, sign posted Hollinsclough. Follow this road for about 300 metres, where you will pass Gauledge farm on your left. Further on, you pass Daisy Knowle farm entrance on your right, and walking downhill you will come to the River Manifold, where there are two houses, one named Dunn Brook Cottage, and the other is Poole Cottage.

Dunn Brook Cottage   Poole Cottage

4) – Continue uphill after passing these two cottages and look on the left for a footpath sign post. A stile here puts you into the field, in which you should aim for the shrub line at the bottom of the field, about 100 metres away from the cottage. It is quite boggy here in places so be careful where you tread. Under the shrubs you will find a stone slab as a bridge over the river, albeit a stream here. Once you have negotiated the bridge into the next field, walk up the hill slope up to a gap in a stone wall. There is also a sign post which reads 'Manifold Trail'.

*(Walk time here – approximately 1 hour 15 minutes.)

5) – Continue walking up the field, heading for a gap in the wall to your right in the corner of the field. Go through this gap and keeping the new wall to your left, walk along the edge of the field, and another gap in a wall puts you alongside Gauledge Farm, which is another building with a grade II listing. Head for a small gate near the corner of the adjoining field, followed by another small wooden gate, and you find yourself on a driveway which forms part of Gauledge Lane on the edge of the village of Longnor.

Gauledge Farm, and the start of Gauledge Lane.

6) – Turn right onto Gauledge Lane, and head down into the village. After about 100 metres or so, on your right is West Bank Cottage, another listed building. Also here is Leigh Cottage, dated 1829, and closely followed by Hill Crest Cottage, making three listed buildings in a row.
    There are further listed buildings here with West Bank House, Bank Cottage, and the large building on the corner is Sheffield House.

7) - Turning around from Sheffield House, walking back past the end of Gauledge Lane, an old house on the corner is notable, which I think is Bank Cottage. Also here are Bakehouse Croft and Spring Cottage, which you pass on the road out of the village, as I head for Longnor Bridge. This is the road back to the Winking Man from where I drove into the village. The road bends around to the right, and then Longnor Bridge comes into view, which is a rebuilt bridge following a flood in 1821. There was a bridge recorded here as early as 1401 and was called Longnor Bridge in 1478.

*(Walk time here – approximately 1 hour and 45 minutes.)

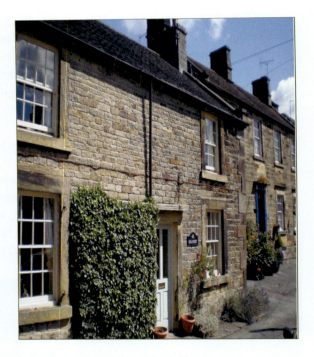

Listed houses in Gauledge Lane, including West Bank Cottage, Leigh Cottage and West Bank House

Sheffield House

Bank Cottage

Longnor Saw Mill

8) - A short walk past the bridge there is a building on the right, which is the converted Longnor saw mill. On the left, before this, is a small road junction. Turn left here and walk along the narrow road for approximately 300 metres to the end, where it meets a larger road. Turn left here and you will be heading back into the village of Longnor, and the view of St. Bartholomew church in the village is quite good from here.

View of Longnor village and St. Bartholomew' church, from Windy Arbour Bridge road

9) - About 250 metres along the road you will come to Windy Arbour Bridge, though I failed to see how it got its name as it was not windy here. The bridge itself, another that has been rebuilt around 1822, seems ordinary and plain. I continue on into the village where the first building to catch the eye is the listed Horseshoe Inn. To the right is another listed inn, the Crewe and Harpur Arms.

Horseshoe Inn   Crewe and Harpur Arms

10) - Walking past the Crewe and Harpur Arms, you can see the archway that leads to the Coachman's House behind, that was used as a stopping place for the horse and coach journeys from Buxton to London in 1803. Directly opposite here is the market house and I imagine the current car park site was where the village market was held. Next to the market house is another listed inn, The Grapes, which in 1860, until 1866, was called 'The Butcher's Arms.

Market House in Longnor village centre, next to the Grapes Inn

*- (Walk time here – approximately 2 ¼ hours)

11) - Continue past The Grapes Hotel, as it is called now, and after 50 metres on the same side is the Cheshire Cheese Inn. Why is it not called the Staffordshire Cheese Inn, as I fail to understand the Cheshire link?

'Ye Olde Cheshire Cheese Inn'.

12) – Just past the inn, on the right-hand side of the road, is a large driveway and a footpath signpost for 'Brund'. The driveway is the entrance to Folds End Farm, another listed building of the village. The next road junction, on the left, is Dove Ridge, which has a sign pointing towards the church. Walk along Dove Ridge, where it meets Church Street, and a few quaint cottages come into view. Among these are listed buildings 'The Cottage', and 'The Old Police House', as well as unlisted Ruby Cottage and Magpie Cottage which I thought were equally pleasant.

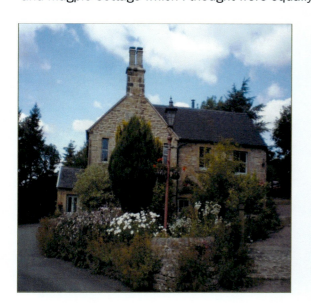

Cottages on Church Street

13) - Walking along Church Street, a small narrow road on the left is Queen Street, where there is an equally impressive row of 'Victoria Cottages', dated 1897. At the bottom of Queen Street is the Grapes Hotel, which gives you an idea of your location in the village.

Victoria Cottages, dated 1897, in Queen Street.

14) - Continuing back along Church Street, more cottages please the eye, and at the end you will come to see St. Bartholomew' Church, with the graveyard to the right on the opposite side of the road, where I discovered an interesting hole in a tree near the gravestones. The gate posts to the church are dated separately with A and 18 on the left post, and D and 33 on the right, i.e. AD1833.

A 'holy' tree (?), in the graveyard of St. Bartholomew' Church.

St. Bartholomew' Church, in Longnor

*- (Walk time – approximately 2 ¾ hours).

15) - The collection of listed buildings in this small area is a lot to take in, with many in Chapel Street just by the church, as well as the Wesleyan Methodist Chapel virtually on the doorstep of St. Bartholomew's. The worn cobble steps in Chapel Street are a delightful sight, and at the bottom is a narrow street passageway which leads back to the market place car park. I spent a good half an hour around this area just admiring the old village buildings.

Listed Buildings in Chapel Street

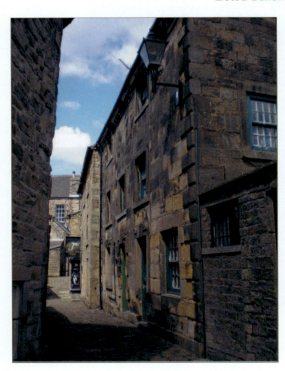

Bottom of Chapel Street

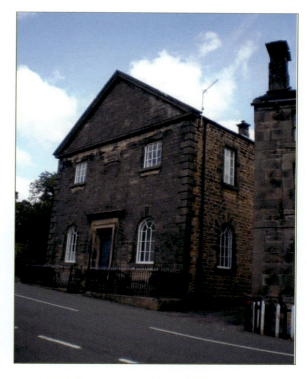

Wesleyan Chapel, built in 1797

16) - After taking in all the village has to offer, I head back along the Buxton road back to the lay-by where I have parked my car. A final glance at the St. Bartholomew' Church as I pass Church Street on my right, and the church affiliated school on my left, serve to stir the thoughts of village life in rural Staffordshire.

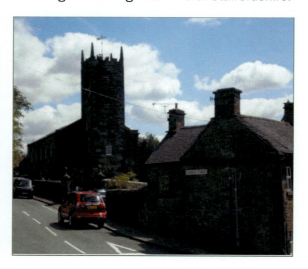

*(Walk time – total, including viewing the village, approximately 3 and ½ hours).

6.1 The Lords of Alstonefield   - The Harpur-Crewe Baronetcy

6.2 Longnor Township   - A Brief History

6.3 History of Medieval Fairs and Markets

6.4 Religion in Longnor

6.5 The Story of St. Bartholomew

View of Longnor village

6.1 *The Lords Of Alstonefield - The 'Harpur – Crewe' Baronetcy

The Lords of Alstonefield - From Gradbach Mill (Walk One) to Longnor (Walk Six)

The Lords of Alstonefield have been mentioned in most of my previous walks, with particular reference to their efforts to promote industry and the provision of religious support in the townships of Quarnford, Heathylee, Hollinsclough, and Fawfieldhead. These efforts continued in the township of Longnor, which is the focus of this next walk, so I take a brief look back into the business dealings of the estate that the Harpur, and Crewe, and Harpur-Crewe families have attended to over the course of time, with a brief glimpse into the influences in the village of Longnor.

On my first walk, I discovered that it was in 1792 that Sir Henry (Harpur) Crewe, the 7th baronet, gave a 31 year lease to three men so as to rebuild Gradbach Mill. Unfortunately, they went bankrupt and the lease was transferred in 1798 to John and Peter Dakeyne in order to continue with employment opportunities in the mill at Gradbach.

On my second walk, Sir John Harpur, the third baronet, gave a lease on a house, thought to be Goldsitch House in Quarnford parish, which was used as a home for coal miners. In 1677 he also gave a lease to a William Wardle to work a coal mine in Quarnford parish.
In 1744, the fifth baronet, Sir Henry Harpur, donated the land that was used to build the original church in Flash village.
In 1765, the sixth baronet, Sir Henry Harpur, gave leases on further coal mining ventures in Quarnford parish.
In 1821, Sir George (Harpur) Crewe, the eighth baronet, provided a house for rent for the curate of Flash church, but this became a little dilapidated by 1840 when finances were directed to other areas.

On my fifth walk, around the townships of 'High Frith', the hard work of the baronets continued. It was noted in 1605, the first baronet, Sir Henry Harpur, had Longnor Mill rebuilt.
In 1764, the 6th baronet, Sir Henry Harpur, gave a lease for a coal mine at Blue Hills in Heathylee township.
In 1820, there was the letter by John Lomas that was sent to Sir George, the eighth baronet, outlining the trials and tribulations of 'hawking' and the building of the Bethel chapel. Sir George also funded the building of the church in Newtown in 1837, as well helping set up the Sunday school in the church in 1841. Sir George also had a barn replaced with the building of St. Agnes church in Hollinsclough, albeit next to John Lomas's Bethel chapel in 1840, and in 1842 the church of Reaps Moor was built with Sir George' help.
In the 1860's, the ninth baronet, Sir John Harpur-Crewe, provided a house called 'The Green', for the curate of Newtown and Reaps Moor to live in. Later in 1884, the ninth baronet also paid for the running costs of the school on the main Leek to Buxton road (opposite the Winking Man pub).

So, onwards I go to Longnor village, for my next walk, and to discover the work of the Lords of Alstonefield there. It was the father of the first baronet, John Harpur, who in 1595 was granted permission by the crown to run a village market in Longnor. This was hardly surprising given that his father, Richard Harpur, was the Justice of the Common Pleas at Westminster.
In 1781, the village pub was named 'The Harpur Arms', after the sixth baronet, Sir Henry Harpur, and was renamed in 1818 as 'The Crewe and Harpur Arms', after the eighth baronet, Sir George. In 1830, Sir George supplied a house for William Buckwell, the curate of St. Bartholomew church, at 'Townend' in Longnor. In 1836, Sir George also noted that the market house needed repairing or rebuilding, but it was his son, the ninth baronet, Sir John Harpur-Crewe, who finally had the market house rebuilt in 1873. So, to finish my walks in this area with Longnor village, there are many links with the Harpur-Crewe family to be found, a pleasant village it is too.

The Lords of Alstonefield

The 'Harpur' baronetcy was a title created on 08th December 1626, for Henry Harpur (c.1579 – 1638), though the Harpur family had a history long before this date. The earliest name to appear in records was that of Richard 'le' Harpur, who became the father of Hugh le Harpur. Hugh le Harpur was given a grant to certain lands around Kenilworth, previously owned by 'canons', in the reign of King Henry I, the youngest son of William the Conqueror. The grant was made at sometime between 1068 and 1135.

During the reign of Edward II, between 1284 and 1327, seven generations after Richard le Harpur, the first member of the Harpur family was knighted. This was Sir Robert le Harpur, who married Isabel Hercy, daughter of Lord Henry Hercy of Pillerton in Warwickshire. The family went on to be linked with knights and barons through marriage for the next three hundred years, when the Harpur baronetcy itself was then created.

The baronetcy was created in the second year of the reign of King Charles I, to the grandson of Richard Harpur, of Swarkestone Hall. Richard had been a successful lawyer and a judge and was given the job of 'Justice of the Common Pleas' at Westminster, from 16 May 1569 until his death on 29 January 1577. This was a title that had been created around 1190, with the first 'Justice of the Common Pleas' named as a Simon of Pattishall. Richard Harpur also had the job of 'Chief Justice of the County Palatine of Lancaster'.

Richard's son, Sir John Harper, was granted the rights to a market in Longnor village by the Crown in 1595, which became a focal point for the community and the name of the Harpur Crewe family for many years. Sir John Harpur married a Jane Findern, and it was their surviving third son, Henry, who was bestowed with the title of the 1st Baronet.

With this title, through wealth and marriage, the family acquired land estates in Derbyshire, Leicestershire and Staffordshire. The family home was at Calke Abbey, although it was never an actual abbey, but it had been an Augustinian priory from the 12th century until the dissolution by Henry VIII. The estate had been purchased in 1622, four years before Sir Henry was given the title of baronet, from a Robert Bainbridge. He was the son of another Robert Bainbridge, who was MP for Derby, and who had been imprisoned in the Tower of London in 1586 for his religious views and 'refusing to accept the Queen's (Elizabeth I) "Church Settlement"'. This had been implemented in 1558 with the 'Act of Supremacy' which re-established the Church of England's separation from Rome, and the 1559 'Act of Uniformity', which outlined the pathway for the Church of England.

The Calke estate was sold to Sir Henry Harpur in 1622 for the sum of £5,350, which in modern day terms amounted to over half a million pounds. The house at Calke was rebuilt into a mansion house between 1701 and 1704, by the fourth baronet, Sir John Harpur (1680-1741), and became the family home for the next 280 years.

The Harpur Baronetcy (established 1626)

1st Baronet -- Sir Henry Harpur (c.1579 – 1639)
2nd Baronet -- Sir John Harpur (1616 – 1669)
3rd Baronet -- Sir John Harpur (1645 – 1681)
4th Baronet -- Sir John Harpur (1679 – 1741)
5th Baronet -- Sir Henry Harpur (1708 – 1748)
6th Baronet -- Sir Henry Harpur (1739 – 1789)
7th Baronet -- Sir Henry (Harpur) Crewe (1763 – 1819)
8th Baronet – Sir George (Harpur) Crewe (1795 – 1844)
9th Baronet -- Sir John Harpur-Crewe (1824 – 1886)
10th Baronet -- Sir Vauncey Harpur-Crewe (1846 – 1924) – died with no male heir.

The seventh baronet, Sir Henry Harpur, changed his name in April of 1808 to Sir Henry Crewe in commemoration of his ancestry, which was in relation to the fourth baronet Sir John Harpur, who had married Catherine Crewe, the daughter of Thomas, the second Lord Crewe. There is also a record that he took up the name and 'arms' of Lord Crewe with a 'royal sign manual' (an authorised signature of the King or Queen).

The seventh baronet was also a controversial man, in that three years after his father's death, he married his mistress, a lady's maid called Ann (or Nanny) Hawkins, in 1792. A marriage that his mother, Lady Frances Greville, described as an 'unfortunate connection'.

The eighth baronet, Sir George (Harpur) Crewe, was the eldest surviving son of the seventh baronet, and succeeded the title after his father had died from a fall from a coach box, on 07th February 1819. Sir George was 24 years old and having been to Rugby School for his education he now inherited Calke 'Abbey', along with extensive properties in Derbyshire, Leicestershire and Staffordshire. He decided to get married later that year in 1819, to a Jane Whitaker, daughter of the Reverend Thomas Whitaker, Vicar of Mendham in Norfolk.

In 1821, he was called upon to serve as High Sheriff of Derbyshire, despite his mother's reputation of being his father's mistress before they married. In contrast to some reports, that he was unduly unconcerned about the tenants of the family estates, he was considered by some to be a philanthropist with strong Christian principles. This was thought to be 'too conscientious' for a member of Parliament, although, after years of taking care of his estates business, he was persuaded to stand as member of Parliament for South Derbyshire in 1835 and was returned as an MP in 1837. His religious views, no doubt helped by the fact that he had married a vicar's daughter, as well as having a good relationship with the curate of Longnor church, William Buckwell, gave rise to the funding of new churches and schools in the Alstonefield estate. However, his health was not good, despite having six children, and he retired as an MP in 1841. He died three years later at the family home of Calke.

His son John, the ninth baronet, was only twenty when he succeeded the baronetcy. He decided to assume the surname of 'Harpur – Crewe', and he became the High Sheriff of Derbyshire in 1853. The last baronet, the tenth, was Sir Vauncey Harpur – Crewe, who was devoted to collecting natural history specimens. He married Jane Henrietta Eliza Lovell, but only had daughters before he died on 13 December 1924, thus leaving the title of the baronetcy to expire.

His grandson, Charles Jenney, took up the name of Charles Harpur-Crewe in 1949 when his aunt Hilda Harpur-Crewe died. She was the eldest sister of his mother, Frances, and thus he inherited the family estate as the eldest male. However, he himself died suddenly in 1981, leaving large death duties of around £8 million to pay. His aunt Hilda had previously had to sell Sir Vauncey's collections of birds, butterflies and fish to pay his death duties, so the Calke estate was transferred to the National Trust in 1985 by Henry Harpur Crewe, who was the younger brother of Charles, as he had no means to pay the duties.

6.2 *Longnor Township - A Brief History

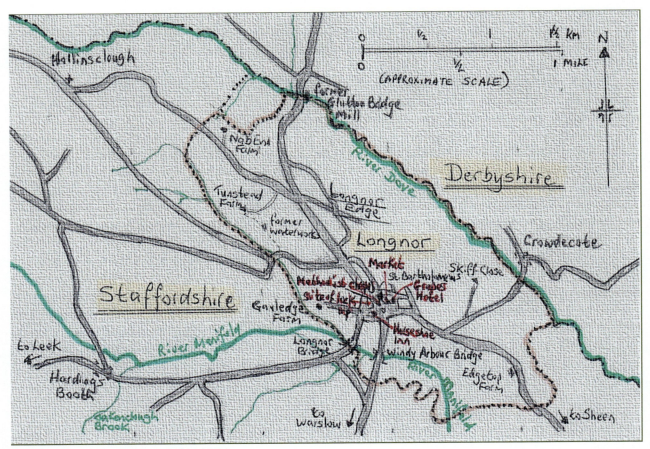

Longnor Township, as recorded in 1994.

In 1227, Longnor village was known as 'Langenoure', which had its name formed from two old English words, 'langen', meaning long, and 'ofer', meaning ridge. The 'long ridge' is now called Longnor Edge, which stretches from Nab End Farm to Edgetop Farm, almost eight kilometres in length. It was subjected to a landslip over time and has a depression which caused damage to the road between Longnor village and Glutton Bridge. At Glutton Bridge itself, on the River Dove, there used to be a mill, built in the 1820's, and was still a working mill until the 1930's. However, it is now a private residence, but there are no signs of the mill workings left, except that the house is called 'Mill House'.

The first record of 'Glutton' was in 1358, when a farm recorded as 'Glotunhous', and was one of the many sheep farms in the Upper Dove area, which all belonged to the estate of the Earl of Lancaster, who gained control of the land just before 1300 from Robert de Ferrers III. The origin of the word 'Glutton' came from a Simon le Gluton of Nottinghamshire, who was first mentioned in 1201, with a possible reference to his apparent over eating habits. Near to the site of Glutton Bridge, there was a cheese making site recorded in 1464, and the cheese that was made there was taken to Longnor village to be stored, close to the site where the Cheshire Cheese Inn is situated. I would be surprised if the cheese was actually anything resembling today's Cheshire cheese though, and technically it is in Staffordshire.

Longnor Edge has its highest point near Nab End Farm, at 1,182 feet (360 metres) above sea level. The ridge dips slightly, as landslips of the sandstone and shalestone rocks below ground caused the land to drop slightly. Longnor village lies at approximately 956 feet (291 metres), before the edge rises again to about 1016 feet (310 metres) at Edge Top Farm. The lowest point in the township area is at 800 feet (244 metres), at the road crossing the River Dove between Longnor and Hartington in Derbyshire.

Longnor township was in the ancient parish of Alstonefield, along with Hollinsclough and Heathylee, Fawfieldhead, Quarnford, and Warslow/Elkstones townships. The north eastern boundary is formed by the River Dove, except a small area in the northern corner, which was land that was claimed by Derbyshire around the 1820's. The south western boundary follows the 'course' of the River Manifold, except at the southern corner which follows the 'old course' of the river. The river ran its natural course in 1770 but was diverted in the 1820's to create a section of canal, but this no longer exists. Population records show that in 1666, only 25 people were living in the township area, and who were assessed for 'hearth tax'. The hearth tax had recently been introduced by the king, Charles II, which was levied for every chimney per house, and was payable twice a year for one shilling. Thus, two shillings a year had to be paid by every household.

A hundred years later, in 1769, there were 58 people in the township 'owing suit' at the manor court, now in the hands of the Harpur baronetcy. A 'suit' was a term used to identify a petition or entreaty made to a person in authority, so in effect it applied to anyone living in the land area who was subject to the law of the landowner. In 1801, and most likely due to the landowners, the Harpur baronetcy, the local population increased to 391. By 1851 it had reached its highest level of 561 inhabitants, but after this there was a steady decline and was as low as 352 inhabitants in 1971.

Despite its slow beginnings, in 1604, Longnor village was described as 'something to be spoken of', as there had been a market set up in the village by John Harpur, the father of the first baronet of the Harpur family, in 1595. There were now ten licensed ale houses recorded in the village, and further inns were to follow with The Horseshoe Inn, dated at 1609, and the Harpur Arms recorded in 1781, which was later changed to the Crewe and Harpur Arms in 1818.There was an inn called the White Horse in 1794 at Townend, to the west side of the market place, and the Harpur Arms itself was used as 'coaching' inn on a route between Buxton and London in 1803. A further five inns were recorded in 1818, including The Bell, the Red Bull, The Swan, and the Cheshire Cheese.

Longnor market had been the reason for this upsurge in demand for alehouses, with the trade centre being a focal point for many travelling traders, hawkers, and pedlars, who would no doubt frequent the local drinking dens to spend their daily profits. Longnor remained an important market village through the 19th century, with several shops opening around the market square, some replacing the less profitable inns. Longnor village also had the attraction of its scenic location, which was described in 1865 as 'quite as beautiful as that of Buxton'. Further inns were recorded, despite some closing down and some being renamed. An inn on the north side of the market was called 'The Board' in 1850 with another inn called 'The Butchers Arms' in 1860, but this was renamed 'The Grapes' in 1866.

Joseph Wain was recorded as being a postman in 1829, and a post office was recorded in 1834. This was run by an Isaac Wain, but it is not known if he was a relative of Joseph. A small branch of the District Bank of Leek was opened in 1864 but was unfortunately closed two years later due to 'an insufficient economy to support it'. Two surgeons were recorded in Longnor in 1813, with both George Fynney and a Frank Wyatt named as living in the area. However, only Mr. Wyatt was still there in 1818. Another surgeon was recorded in 1834, with a William Flint living in the area until 1851. Later in the 1870's and 1880's, there was a surgeon recorded with the name of Joseph Poole in Longnor.

New houses were being built on the east side of the village in 1837, with a row of four cottages near Townhead Farm. Also, a row of six cottages were built in Queen Street, dated 1897, known as Victoria Cottages. There is one house in Chapel Street dated 1774. Earlier than that, there is the site of the Fold End Farm, also to the east of the village, that was recorded as occupied in 1505, with another house on the west side of the village at Gauledge recorded in 1608. The road that leads from the village heading towards Leek crosses the River Manifold. There was a bridge recorded there in 1401, and was known in 1478 as Longnor Bridge, possibly after having been rebuilt. The bridge itself was definitely rebuilt in 1822, after a flood washed it away the year before. Glutton Bridge and Windy Arbour Bridge were also rebuilt around this time.

Longnor - Local Governance, the Village Fairs and the Market

As part of the medieval system of a self-policing and self-governing society, Longnor formed a 'tithing' in Alstonefield Manor, and by 1400 it had a 'frankpledge'. In 1500, Longnor had its own six-man jury at the manor court, and two years later this became a twelve-man jury. In April 1505, the jury met up with its counterpart from nearby Warslow to form a 'great court'. However, this was only ever repeated once more, in 1550, with the rest of the time spent as separate frankpledge units.

Stocks were present in the village, as mentioned in 1601, and again in 1614, with a new pair of stocks recorded in 1861. In 1831, there was a record of bull baiting in the market place, which came as part of 'wakes week'. Longnor 'wakes' had begun in August of 1697, probably to celebrate the feast of St. Bartholomew. From 1772, the 'wakes' were held in September, which later incorporated pony trotting and horse races, along with less energetic pastimes such as 'well-dressings'.

In 1595, the Crown had granted John Harpur a Tuesday Market in Longnor, and in the 1770's there was a proposal to build a market house. The original building contractor chosen was a Richard Gould, but he unfortunately went bankrupt in 1773. However, the market house was eventually built in 1817, but was noted as needing to be repaired, or rebuilt, by Sir George (Harpur) Crewe in 1836. It was eventually rebuilt in 1873 by his son, Sir John (Harpur) Crewe. In 1931, the market house became a social hall for the parish and was known as Longnor village hall in 1940.

Fairs had been held in the village since 1293, usually in the space around the church of St. Bartholomew. There were four 'fairs' recorded in Longnor by 1549, and these were acquired by John Harpur prior to his market grant of 1595. In 1817, there were eight fairs recorded, including those on Easter Tuesday, two fairs in May, Whit Tuesday, and one on Candlemas Day which is normally forty days after Christmas Day.

Longnor was one of the few places in Staffordshire to have a hiring fair in the early 20th century and is also home to the annual 'Longnor Sports' (or Wakes) Races. Traditionally, these were started in 1904, held on the first Thursday after the first Sunday in September, at Waterhouse Farm. It starts with a gymkhana, followed by a series of harnessed-horse races, and then there is a 'Golden Mile' fun run and a cross country hill race.

Entrance of Longnor market building

6.3 *History of Medieval Fairs and Markets.

Medieval fairs and markets in England required a franchise, which was only given by right of a grant from the Crown or the authority of parliament, before they were allowed to be set up. The demand for fairs and markets were partly due to the trading problems of travelling to obtain certain special goods. Travelling tradesmen faced constant dangers from highwaymen, and villagers were less likely to travel long distances for goods they required. Public gatherings, especially for religious but also judicial and military reasons, brought together the scattered population of the townships, and these occasions were seen as opportunities for commerce that gave an ideal location for a fair or market.

The origin of the word 'fair' comes from the Latin word 'feria', meaning a 'holy day'. Each 'feria' was a day when large numbers of people would assemble for worship. The Church took an active part in sponsoring fairs on 'feast' days, and as a result fairs became an important source of revenue funding for the Church. Commerce, by way of the Medieval fairs and religion became closely entwined.

It was only after the Norman Conquest that fairs in England became an important part of the village, and indeed the country as a whole. Early records show that from 1199 to 1483 there were approximately 2800 grants of franchise markets and fairs in England. More than half of these were granted during the reigns of King John (1166-1216) and his successor King Henry III (1207-1272), which is also the period of a rising power of the Church.

The first recorded grant was made by either William the Conqueror, or his son William Rufus, to the Bishop of Winchester, to hold a 'free fair' at St. Giles Hill, between 1066 and 1100. This became the biggest fair in Europe, lasting sixteen days, when all the revenues from the fair were held by the Church instead of going to the Crown as was normally the case. In 1248, Henry III granted a similar privilege to the abbot of Westminster in return for 'translation' of Edward the Confessor.

Medieval fairs in Europe were generally held during the period of a saint's 'feast', and usually in the precincts of the church or abbey. In England, however, this was seen as a desecration of a church, or churchyard, and was therefore forbidden during the reign of Edward I (1239-1307). Medieval fairs in England were then held on village greens, or on open land near to, or within, the village. They were not permanent sites, and merchants would set up their wares in temporary tents, or 'booths'. Although the main objective of the 'fair' was to trade goods, almost every fair contained some element of merry-making, sometimes in the form of bull baiting, and a variety of acrobats, jugglers, sword-swallowers, and wrestlers. Some even had jousting events, and horse races, along with dancing bears and performing monkeys.

Medieval fairs were much bigger than markets, although they happened less often than markets, with some merchants travelling huge distances on foot, or on horseback, from one fair to the next. The wares that were sold at fairs varied more than those at a market, and especially precious metals and gems, silk and spices, and perfumes were more likely to appear at a fair.

As more people were settling in townships, they were growing their own food and making their own clothes, and many were farming animals, which all led to excesses of wares and food and animals that could be sold at a local market, preferably so that they could return home at the end of the same day. Crafts people found it advantageous to build workshops close to market places, which in turn helped the villages to form and grow. Many original markets were set up at road crossings or river bridges, before a small village would start to be formed. Sundays grew to be a popular day for a market in Medieval England, as local people would attend church before visiting the market to 'socialize'. Many markets were originally organised by churches, and local landowners, to encourage trade and population growth. In some markets there were people paid to check on weights and measurements, and quality of goods, with anyone found guilty of an infringement likely to be put in the local stocks and pelted with rotten fruit and vegetable by disgruntled customers.

6.4 *Religion In Longnor

A church in Longnor village was first recorded in 1448, with the first church wardens recorded in 1553. The church that is seen today, was dedicated to the name of St. Bartholomew around 1631, but is one that was built, following the demolition of a previous church between 1774 and 1781, on a site slightly north of the original. The new Church of St. Bartholomew had an upper arcade of windows built on the west and south galleries in 1812, and also had the west tower increased in height at the same time. A font, believed to be of Norman origin, was found in the churchyard in 1830, and the archdeacon ordered that it should be placed into the new church. However, this had not been done until seven years later. The existence of the font suggested that an original church at Longnor may have existed in the 12th century, but only the plans of the church demolished by 1781 are known to exist.

The stone gate posts at the entrance to the walkway to the church are dated 1833 and were part of the improvements implemented by the curate William Buckwell, who was newly appointed in 1830. He became good friends with the current Lord of Alstonefield, Sir George (Harpur) Crewe, who had a house rebuilt at Townend in 1831 for the curate to live in. With William Buckwell as the curate of Longnor church in 1830, there was only the one weekly Sunday service, with Communion being celebrated four times a year. On the census Sunday of 1851 there were two Sunday services, with an attendance in the morning of 135 people, and an evening service attended by 126 township residents.

Much earlier, in 1549, the curate of the old church was recorded as being entitled to payment from the village fairs. A payment of one penny for every booth used, and a half penny for each booth unused, at each of Longnor's four fairs, amounted to a total of approximately four shillings a year. In the next century, in 1644, a parliamentary committee awarded the curate, Anthony Gretton, a salary of £5. This was to be paid by the estate of Sir John Harpur, the second baronet of Alstonefield. In 1733, the inhabitants of Longnor 'chapelry' agreed to make payments in order to secure the residence of Joseph Bradley, who was the curate chosen by them with the approval of the vicar of Alstonefield. These payments were to be made for seven years, or until grants were paid by the governors of the 'Queen Anne Bounty', which was a fund set up in 1704 to pay the poorer clergy from the taxes collected by the Crown from all of the clergy of the Church of England. Grants were made in 1737 and in 1751 to the value of £200, which meant that the curate was taking an average salary of £10 per year. In 1775, Sir Henry Harpur, the sixth baronet, agreed to pay the curate £7 and 10 shillings, on top of another £200 grant that was made by the governors in the following year.

The townships of Fawfieldhead, Heathylee, Hollinsclough and Quarnford, all came under the 'chapelry' of Longnor in the late 17th century. A chapelry was a term used for a subdivision of a parish, which in most cases were similar to a township, except that a chapelry referred to a subdivision that had a place of worship within its domain. The parish of Alstonefield thus had its chapelry of Longnor, at least until 1744, when the church of St. Paul was built in Flash village. Longnor itself was made a parish in 1902, which incorporated the township of Longnor, along with most of Fawfieldhead township, and the eastern halves of Hollinsclough and Heathylee townships. The western halves of the latter became part of the parish of Quarnford, with St. Paul's church in Flash being the parish's place of worship.

Non-conformist Religious Following in Longnor

In 1685, a Longnor man recorded as Elihu Hall, who is possibly the same man recorded as Elijah Hall in 1723, registered his house as a meeting place for Quakers. In 1731, a registered Quaker by the name of James Plant was also recorded as the 'headborough' for Longnor township.

The first recorded Quakers lived in mid – 17th century England, so the Quaker movement would have been in its infancy in 1685 with Elihu Hall as a follower in Longnor. Their message was based on the religious belief that "Christ has come to teach his people himself" and stressed the importance of a direct relationship with God through Jesus Christ. They also had the philosophy that a direct religious belief would be part of a universal 'priesthood' for all believers. This philosophy was emphasized by having a personal direct religious experience of Christ which was acquired through the reading and studying of the Bible. Quakers would focus their private lives on the development of their behaviour and speech reflecting emotional purity and the 'light of God'. The movement arose from dissenting Protestant groups who wanted to break away from the 'established' Church of England.

Quakers were known for their use of the word 'thou' as part of normal speech. They were also known for their refusal to take part in wars, and with an opposition to slavery. They were also renowned for wearing plain clothes and for being teetotal, i.e. no consumption of alcohol. Some Quakers were recorded in the setting up of well - known banks and companies, including Barclays Bank, Lloyds Bank, Cadbury's Chocolate Co., Fry's and Rowntree's. They are also known for their activities in seeking abolition of slavery and prison reform.

In 1769, a group of Methodist followers met at the home of a Mr. Billing, and there was a private prayer meeting in 1772 led by John Wesley, as mentioned in the Flash Methodist following, which was attended by 18 people. By 1784, Longnor had its own Methodist society, with a membership of 42 people recorded. There was a Methodist chapel at the Top o' the Edge farm site to the east of the village, but this was replaced in 1797 with the present building in the centre of the village at Chapel Street. Sunday services were held there every fortnight in 1798, and from 1802 they were weekly services. The attendance on census Sunday of 1851 was recorded as 30 in the afternoon, and 70 in the evening.

The Wesleyan chapel was enlarged in 1853, with the building of galleries, and the front of the chapel totally rebuilt. It was closed as a place of worship in 1993 but was being used as a shop and a 'doll hospital', with much of the original furniture, pulpit, pews, and choir stalls still inside the building.

Wesleyan Chapel in Longnor (with St. Bartholomew's tower behind)

6.5 *The Story of Saint Bartholomew

Bartholomew is from a Greek name, 'Bartholomaios', which in turn was derived from an Aramaic name of 'bar-Tolmay'. This Aramaic name is said to mean 'son of the furrows', with a reference to farming. The name of Bartholomew that became a saint, is one of the 'Twelve Apostles of Jesus Christ' that is listed in the Bible in three of the four Gospels, namely Matthew, Mark, and Luke. In each of these Gospels, Bartholomew is mentioned in the company of Philip, who was also named as one of the 'twelve apostles', and it is said that he introduced Bartholomew to Jesus. Bartholomew was born in Cana, Galilee.

There are two ancient testimonies from the 4th Century that refer to missions that were made by Bartholomew in India. Testimonies by Saint Jerome, and another by Eusebius of Caesarea, refer to visits to the Bombay region of India, where Bartholomew was trying to spread the Gospel of Matthew, and Christianity. Bartholomew also made visits to parts of Ethiopia and Mesopotamia, and finally to Armenia, where unfortunately he met his ill-fated death.

He was travelling with a fellow apostle, Jude Thaddeus, in the first century, when it was reputed that Bartholomew was spreading the message of Christianity into Armenia. As a result, both Jude and Bartholomew are considered as patron saints of the Armenian Apostolic Church. It was Bartholomew that was held responsible for converting King Polymius of Armenia to the Christian faith, and in so doing he angered the king's brother, Astyages – who consequently ordered the execution of Bartholomew.

There are at least three differing accounts of how Bartholomew was killed. One speaks of him being beaten until he was unconscious before being thrown into the sea to drown, whilst a second account tells of him being crucified in an upside-down position. A third account has become the most favoured, which tells the story of Bartholomew being skinned alive before being beheaded in Albac, or Albanopolis, in Armenia. This location is now in south eastern Turkey, near to a town called Baskale.

Following this final account of his death, Bartholomew was judged to have been made a 'martyr', having suffered a painful death in the cause of Christianity, and was consequently declared a saint. There is a 13th Century 'Monastery of St. Bartholomew', which was constructed to commemorate the site of his death, which was then in the Vasparukan Province of Greater Armenia.

His death is also commemorated in other faiths, though they are held on different dates, with the 'Feast of St. Bartholomew' held by the Eastern Christianity followers on June 11th, with the same 'Feast' being held on August 24th by the Anglican Communion and the Catholic Church. The Coptic Orthodox Church commemorates his martyrdom on the 1st day of the Coptic Calendar – which currently falls on September 11th (and corresponds to August 29th in the Gregorian calendar).

In the Eastern Christian Church, where Bartholomew's evangelical labours were supposedly carried out, he is identified as 'Nathanael'. However, Nathanael is only mentioned in the Gospel of John. In the Synoptic Gospels, as mentioned earlier, Philip and Bartholomew are always mentioned together, whereas Nathanael is never mentioned, which leads some bodies rejecting the idea that Nathanael is identified as Bartholomew.

Many 'miracles' are associated with Bartholomew, both before and after his death. A few of these miracles are particularly celebrated by the townsfolk of a small island off the coast of Sicily, called Lipari. The existence of so called 'relics' at Lipari, which was under the rule of Constantinople at the time of Bartholomew's death, are thought to be explained by the body of Bartholomew being washed up on the shore of the island. A large piece of skin and some bones were kept in the Cathedral of St. Bartholomew on Lipari. The relics were held in a state of conservation at the basilica of San Bartolomeo all Isola, which had been an old pagan medical centre. For this reason, the name of Bartholomew was then associated with medicine, and most notably in London with the hospital affectionately known as St. Bart's.

Epilogue

When you look at a map book to plan a walk, everything is flat, and dry, and all the marked routes of footpaths and roads seem so straightforward enough as to give the impression that there would not be too much effort involved. Even the distances on a map seem to be easily achievable, but this is where the reality kicks in when you are out there walking. You slowly realise that a mile on the map may actually be a mile and a half of steep uphill climbing, and the energy expended physically is then found to be far more than the energy used to plan the walk, and ultimately a four mile walk on paper is actually nearer six miles on the ground.

However, these facts were not a deterrent after the mishaps and miscalculations of my first walk. It is easy to criticise in hindsight, but I wanted to think that I was something of an intrepid explorer into unknown territory. Even with a map book for guidance, I still managed to get a sense of how it might have been for the first settlers in 'virgin' territory. The terrain of the Staffordshire Moorlands, as the name itself suggests, is mainly barren soggy moorland, with patches of remaining woodland and rivers to negotiate amongst the rolling hills and craggy rock outcrops. Some of the moorland has been converted into farming land, and though many old bridleways still exist, new footpaths and modern day tracks and roads have been etched into the landscape to make the task of exploration a little easier, although at times this did not help when faced with frustration and fatigue.

It seemed at first glance, that much of my planning to explore all of Staffordshire was going to be quite straightforward to complete. But, after six walks of somewhat gruelling reality checks, it soon became apparent that I would have to scale down my expectations. Nonetheless, my endeavours became hugely rewarding to me, as my exploits from village to village threw up untold amounts of useful, or useless, information, depending on which way you look at it, with the help of that modern day encyclopaedia that is the internet. At least I can honestly say that I have trodden the paths of time and enjoyed most of them!

The River Dane, and Danebridge, may have seemed an unlikely place to start. Actually, my original plans were to start at Flash, which is the most northern village in Staffordshire, as well as being the highest 'village' in England and the disputed highest 'village' in Great Britain. As I had made some plans for at least three walks it was only on the first day that I chose to start at Danebridge. This was prompted, for no other reason than it appeared to have a slightly more scenic attraction than Flash, and my mind was set on visiting Lud's 'Church' gorge as my first major geological conquest. Though there was the unplanned conquest of firstly Black Brook, and then the Roaches Ridge, which did initially dampen the spirits before I eventually got to Lud's Church.

The walk itself changed the way I was to approach my recording of subsequent walking plans. A simple record of each twist and turn along the way was not the most inspiring of reading material, and the discoveries of historical facts about the area and its buildings that I saw 'en route' made much more appealing reading to me. It soon became apparent that a small 'booklet' of walks was going to be a much bigger affair as I set about expanding my own knowledge of local history.

As each walk unfolded, I was surprised at how much effort I had to put in to get a fuller picture of the environment I found myself in. My research did not prepare myself for that, and it is only when making the connections between information on paper and the physical reality on the ground that you really get a sense of personal satisfaction and achievement.

So, to start summarizing a little, my discoveries of a rare sheep breeding farm in the setting of Back Forest, along with the old mill sites including that at Gradbach along the banks of the River Dane, were a brief insight into the history of settlement in the area from the present to the past. The geological interest came with a steep climb up to the top of the Roaches, the Hanging Stone, and climaxed with the gorge of Lud's Church. Further interest came in the form of legendary tales of knights linked to the gorge, and other stories of knights appear in areas visited later.

Footpath to the top of the Roaches at Roach End Farm

At Flash village, I got a different feeling, with a realisation of how remote some settlements are. Research into early settlers, coal mining, and religion in the area gave me a slight sense of foreboding. But, only to the extent that the harsh surroundings must have put the fear of God into those first intrepid settlers here, and it is no surprise that they felt the need to seek some religious guidance to continue living there. Considering also that living from hand to mouth under the rule of some tyrannical landlords would have been a difficult life to lead with the best of working conditions. I can only imagine the hardships they must have faced.

Onwards then to Rushton Spencer, where my feelings towards religion became more intensified with the variety of guidance being offered and sought. I found the mixture of a conformist Catholicism and Protestantism, with non-conformist Methodism and even Paganism a possibility, all leading to a confusion of understanding its progression. Links to the past were often found in the present, and in some cases a link comes back full circle to some previous discoveries. This gave rise to connections from churches to railways, villages to landlords, and technology advances in mills and canals, all linked back to geological formations of the moorlands, and even an occasional wallaby sighting thrown in.

On my fifth walk, my attentions were turned back to the Roaches, with the Winking Man, and to Flash village, but this time heading east down the River Dove and River Manifold valleys. The atmosphere of the surroundings has a slightly different feel, with its leaning to a more agricultural environment. That said, there is still the religious connection from the Dane valley, but with a different development of lifestyle because of a new approach from the landlords, the Harpur-Crewe family and the Lords of Alstonefield. They were in contrast to the Brocklehurst baronetcy of the Danebridge and Heaton estates. With the economies of the clothing and paper mills dominating the River Dane, there was the contrasting agricultural village life of Hollinsclough and Longnor in the valleys of the Dove and the Manifold. The introduction of the village market in Longnor saw a big change in the development of settlements and population behaviour in the area, and as the surge in alcoholic intake increased there was the steadying hand of religion.

So, my investigations end with a final religious story looking at the life of a saint, that of Saint Bartholomew. A life that began with the guidance of Jesus Christ, but one that ended with a sense of rejection and suffering. This is portrayed with a story that depicts skin and bone as uncomfortable reading material, and so after attending to my own skin and bone complaints, with blisters and bruises as proof of my punishment, I look forward to my next endeavours. I peruse my map book and head for South Staffordshire, where I begin my next set of planned walks, starting with the village of Kinver. Only fourteen map pages down, and with two hundred and sixty or so to go, there is so much still to discover in Staffordshire. I hope you enjoyed this 'booklet', and I will endeavour to continue my education in the next.

Acknowledgements

I would like to thank my wife for her patience in respect to the reams of paperwork scattered in our home, and to her sister, and her husband, for encouragement to continue with my exploits and writing. Most of my information would not have been possible without research done on internet sites, to which I would like to list, as below, the many sites that I found very useful, and I pass on my many thanks to their producers.

Guide References and Research Information Sources

Phillips Ordnance Survey Street Atlas, Staffordshire - ISBN 0-540-08117-5

Walking With Wordsworth in the Lake District (Norman & June Buckley) - ISBN 978-0-7112-2931-0

www.british-history.ac.uk/vch/staffs/vol7
www.peakdistrictinformation.com/towns/wincle.php
www.britishlistedbuildings.co.uk/en-58159-danebridge
www.peakdistrictinformation.com/features/dane.php
https://en.wikipedia.org/wiki/Soay-sheep
https://en.wikipedia.org/wiki/Boreray-sheep
https://en.wikipedia.org/wiki/Lud's-Church
www.peakdistrictinformation.com/visits/ludschurch.php
www.gradbachscoutcamp.org.uk
www.nulc.ac.uk/gradbach
https://en.wikipedia.org/wiki/Sir-Gawain-and-the-Green-Knight
www.backforest.co.uk
www.backdane.co.uk
www.theknightstable.co.uk
www.cybergata.com/roots/2253.htm (Piers le Clerc de Thornton)
www.go4awalk.com>oliverhill
https://en.wikipedia.org/wiki/Flash,-Staffordshire
https://en.eikipedia.org/wiki/River-Manifold
www.british-history.ac.uk/vch/staffs/vol7/pp49-56
www.methodistheritage.org.uk
https://en.wikipedia.org/wiki/John-Wesley
https://en.wikipedia.org/wiki/Hugh-Despenser-the-Younger
www.british-history.ac.uk/vch/staffs/vol7/Quarnford
https://en.wikipedia.org/wiki/Rushton-Staffordshire
www.rushtonspencer.info/Pages/ParishHome.htm
www.knotinnrushton.pub
https://en.wikipedia.org/wiki/Lawrence-of-Rome
www.mondrem.net/myths/Thomas-Meaykin.html
www.methodistheritage.org.uk/cloudmethodistchapel.htm
www.britishlistedbuildings.co.uk/england/staffordshire/rushton
www.megalithic.co.uk/article.php (The Bridestones)
https://en.wikipedia.org/wiki/Churnet-Valley-Line
https://en.wikipedia.org/wiki/Rushton-railway-station
www.rushton-manor.org.uk/history
www.british-history.ac.uk/vch/staffs/vol7/Rushton

https://en.wikipedia.org/wiki/Rudyard-Lake
www.rudyardlake.co.uk/lake-canals/archive
www.wincle.org.uk/history-mill.html
https://en.wikipedia.org/wiki/Hollander-beater
https://en.wikipedia.org/wiki/Brocklehurst-baronets
www.roaches.org/uk
www.stokesentinel.co.uk/Wallabies-roaming-Roaches
www.british-history.ac.uk/vch/staffs/vol7/Leek
www.etheses.whiterose.ac.uk/3429/1/251292-VOL1.pdf
www.british-history.ac.uk/vch/staffs/vol7/Alstonefield
www.poemhunter.com>Poems (Robert Southey-Mary the Maid)
www.thebmc.co.uk>RockClimbingHuts (Don Whillans Hut)
www.hollinsclough.org.uk/localhistory3.htm (John Lomas)
https://en.wikipedia.org/wiki/Bethel
https://en.wikipedia.org/wiki/Jacob's-Ladder
www.hollinsclough.staffs.sch.uk/Flexi.htm
https://en.wikipedia.org/wiki/Harpur-Crewe-baronets
www.british-history.ac.uk/vch/staffs/vol7/Longnor
www.british-history.ac.uk/vch/staffs/vol7/Fawfieldhead
www.british-history.ac.uk/vch/staffs/vol7/Heathylee
www.medieval-life-and-times.info/fairs
www.britishlistedbuildings.co.uk/england/staffordshire/longnor
https://en.wikipedia.org/wiki/Longnor-Staffordshire
https://en.wikipedia.org/wiki/Bartholomew-the-Apostle